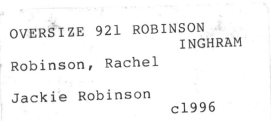

JACKIE ROBINSON

An Intimate Portrait

JACKIE ROBINSON

An Intimate Portrait

BY RACHEL ROBINSON

WITH LEE DANIELS

FOREWORD BY ROGER WILKINS

HARRY N. ABRAMS, INC., PUBLISHERS

EDITOR: SHARON AVRUTICK
DESIGNER: RAYMOND P. HOOPER
PHOTO EDITOR: JOHN K. CROWLEY

PAGE 2: *No one knows exactly when this picture—
the only existing photo of Jack as a young child—was taken.
It hung in his mother's living room in Pasadena.*

Library of Congress Cataloging-in-Publication Data
Robinson, Rachel, 1922–
Jackie Robinson : an intimate portrait / by Rachel Robinson with
Lee Daniels : foreword by Roger Wilkins.
p.   cm.
Includes bibliographical references and index.
ISBN 0–8109–3792–1 (clothbound)
1. Robinson, Jackie, 1919–1972.   2. Afro-American baseball
players—Biography.   3. Brooklyn Dodgers (Baseball team)—History.
I. Daniels, Lee.   II. Title.
GV865.R6R592   1996
769.357'092—dc20
[B]   96–14499

Published in 1996 by Harry N. Abrams, Incorporated, New York
A Times Mirror Company

Printed and bound in Japan

or

Jack and Jackie,

Mallie Robinson, and Raymond and Zellee Isum

—our loved ones, who left us a better,

though still-challenging world to deal with—

and

for Sharon and David, my grandchildren,

and Mack and Willa Mae and their families

—who remain to carry on in a spirit

of belief and wholesome struggle—

and

for the Jackie Robinson Scholars, who carry

the torch of inspiration into world communities

Contents

On the New York Giants opening day in the spring of 1944, patriotic bunting decorated the idiosyncratic old Polo Grounds, and the flags flew high on the poles over the ball yard down on Eighth Avenue just below Coogan's Bluff. I lived on Sugar Hill, the "affluent" part of Harlem, from which you could look down and, from some vantage points, peer through structural openings and actually see part of right field.

On great busy days like this one, fans from New Jersey would park all over our part of Sugar Hill, and we Harlem kids would pester them as they got out of their vehicles with the insistent query:

"Park your car for you, mister?"

We weren't running a valet service, of course, but something more like a naked protection racket. In exchange for a quarter we would—by implication—"guarantee" that no hoodlum would damage the man's car. That day I heard one of my customers express what must have been a common view of us as he explained the transaction to one of his riders just after he had watched me leap to catch the quarter he had negligently flipped in my direction.

"It's worth a quarter to watch these little pickaninnies scramble," he said.

After we had done our scrambling, my pals and I would most likely go down to a local movie house and see big white men winning the war and romancing beautiful white women. We weren't in the pictures of real life just as we weren't inside the glorious apartments and restaurants downtown which were often portrayed in those movies and which we could glimpse from the outside while only imagining the rich joy that came from being part of that life. And, of course, we weren't on the baseball diamond down at the Polo Grounds either.

When we did see an occasional portrayal of our people on the screen, it was as a dim-witted, tangle-tongued, shuffling clown or a big fat mammy whose lifelong obsession was to preserve the comfort and enhance the well-being of the white folks whom she served so faithfully and with such good cheer.

I was twelve then, and the culture came at me every day of my life. I came from a strong, proud family, but they couldn't completely obliterate the lessons that our nation pressed so incessantly upon my soul. I believed that I should be treated equally, but deep in some secret places down inside, I *knew* I was inferior. Everything good, decent, powerful, and beautiful in the world was white, and we were the people who lived in the leftover part of town as the afterthoughts of a good, powerful, thrusting democratic country. We were expected to be grateful for what we had and to imitate life and to support the white heroes who were permitted to fight the war under the leadership of our white president and our white generals. And when it came to the sports that Americans took seriously—particularly baseball, which was at the center of national consciousness in those days—we had to root for the white fellows or settle for black baseball, which didn't have as much money and therefore didn't present as clean and grand a spectacle.

Three years after that opening day, Jack Roosevelt Robinson took over first base for the Brooklyn Dodgers and shredded the white construct that had been imposed on me and my friends and on all our black ancestors from the day in August 1619 when twenty blacks were sold to the Jamestown colony off a visiting Dutch man-of-war. For the first time, we had a black man at the center of white consciousness to root for. And he wasn't one of those almost-white black people either. He was a man whose skin was the color that, on others, caused even blacks to target them with scorn and ridicule. Jack Roosevelt Robinson was a *black* man and very beautiful. He was also excellent, in all respects.

Before Jack came to the Dodgers, America really hadn't acknowledged—over any length of time—full black heroes. There, of course, had been some dancers, singers, and musicians who had achieved celebrity among certain segments of the cognoscenti, but they were not national figures. Then, as Nazi darkness began descending on Europe, three blacks, whose moments in the spotlight undoubtedly made Jack's entry onto the national stage more likely, flashed into national consciousness.

The first was Jesse Owens, the superb track athlete who won four gold medals at the 1936 Berlin Olympics in a glorious set of performances that embarrassed Hitler and gave the lie to his master-race theory. But with no further vehicle available to him, Owens soon faded from view. Then, in 1937, Joe Louis, the Brown Bomber of Detroit, destroyed the German champion Max Schmeling in less than two minutes of the first round. Even whites who hated blacks, but were patriotic and despised the Nazis, loved Louis for that. Though he had a long and distinguished career as heavyweight champion and held captive virtually every black heart in the nation, Louis was, in the end, only a boxer and an unlettered man who still spoke the language of his parents, that of the Alabama cotton fields. Many whites loved him as a kind of national pet. Finally, there was the great contralto Marian Anderson, who sang at the Lincoln Memorial in 1939 after the Daughters of the American Revolution denied her the opportunity to perform at Constitution Hall. Americans of all colors continued to pay homage to Anderson's enormous talent and great dignity all the rest of her life, but only for that one moment was she at the center of national consciousness.

But the general acclaim accorded to those three extraordinary people lingered over the United States as it fought a war to vindicate human freedom with a segregated army. The achievements of Owens, Louis, and Anderson had begun to suggest the human richness that lay under the popular stereotypes of blacks. The myriad of opportunities for human interaction—even in our segregated forces—during the war amplified those lessons a hundred thousandfold. There were millions of white Americans, of course, who did not miss the unbearable ironies presented by our master-race–based society struggling idealistically to defeat the great demon of a European master-race theorist.

Joe Louis and the Negro baseball leagues taught yet one more powerful lesson. The Negro leagues demonstrated for all who had nonideological eyes for talent that blacks could surely play great baseball and that black fans were willing to pay to see it. Joe Louis proved that even white people were willing to pay to see superior black athletes in action. Neither lesson was lost on Branch Rickey, the Calvinistic old capitalist who was running the postwar Dodgers.

Nobody, however, could have been prepared for the 1947 triumph and ordeal of Jack Robinson and his wife, Rachel. Rickey had done what he could to prepare Robinson for what he would encounter on the ballfield and had ordered him to steel himself not to react to the racist bile that would be heaped on him. From that and his year in the minor leagues, Robinson had some idea of what was coming, but to say that baseball was not ready for Robinson would be to understate the case by thousands of country miles. Robinson's minor-league manager had asked Rickey if he truly thought "a nigger is really a human being." Bob Feller, the great Cleveland Indians pitcher and equally great selfregarder, expressed the view that Robinson did not possess the physique of a major leaguer and, but for his race, wouldn't have been considered a serious prospect. Three of Robinson's prospective Dodger teammates tried to petition management to keep him off the team.

But it was on the field in competition that Robinson really met the mixture of white and baseball culture. Fear is central to baseball—fear of beaning, fear of being spiked, fear of dramatic individual failure—opportunities for which baseball provides in abundance. There are also the grating, needling insults designed to wither the spirits of a tender competitor and hasten his failures. "Nigger" and "snowflake" were simply the preludes to the vilest insults that some of America's crudest minds could devise. Robinson endured all of this—in spades, if you will, and in silence. Ultimately, his team jelled around him, and with dignity and brilliance, he played a dazzling season, hit .297, and was voted Rookie of the Year.

It is very hard to be a rookie and be forced to answer by deed again and again, over the course of a long season, the question of whether one has major-league skills. Some players simply crack under the strain. Robinson faced that, the fierce hostility of many, and he had another huge burden as well. On the day he signed with the Dodgers, the *Boston Chronicle* ran a headline screaming: "TRIUMPH OF WHOLE RACE SEEN IN JACKIE'S DEBUT IN MAJOR LEAGUE BALL." Robinson was a smart fellow. He could imagine another headline in September: "FAILURE OF WHOLE RACE SEEN IN JACKIE'S DISMAL SEASON." All eyes were on him. Virtually every American male had played some form of baseball or other and had cherished heroic World Series fantasies. Robinson was in everybody's consciousness, and he knew it, and he carried his whole race on his shoulders through the 154 games of April, May, June, July, August, and Sep-

tember. There has never been a baseball achievement like it, and surely no baseball wife has ever been called upon to share deeper anguish or greater but endlessly demanding triumph than Rachel Robinson did in 1947.

It was only after Rickey took the wraps off him in his third year that we began to get the full measure of this man and of the internal costs the discipline of his year in the minors and first two in the majors must have cost him. Robinson was deeply intelligent and sensitive. He was a fierce race man to the core and as proud and competitive a human being as ever walked the earth. He struck back on the ballfield, rejected any segregation that was imposed on him off the field, and demonstrated such a militant spirit about race matters generally that some whites who formerly had admired him now became critics. They thought it was his job to play ball and then shut up, and they resented the fact that he had opinions and the mind and courage to present them. Many of these people, some of them influential sportswriters, much preferred his enormously talented black Dodger teammate, the mild-mannered catcher Roy Campanella.

But if the controlled Robinson of the early years had been a brilliant path-breaking baseball star, the full-throated fiercely proud, fiercely competitive, fiercely black man of his later years secured his stature as one of the greatest Americans of the twentieth century. When he strode alone into the national spotlight, the country was still in the grips of the postslavery caste system that the South had imposed and the North had condoned ever since the end of Reconstruction in early 1877. Any resistance to the requirements of racial etiquette could result in disaster for blacks, as Lieutenant Jack Robinson had found out when he had refused to move to the back of a military bus during his time in the Army and was court-martialed for it. Blacks were still segregated in the South, and huge numbers of them were relegated to semislavery in the cotton fields. In the urban South and in the North, most blacks were shunted off to the worst jobs the economy provided, and their children got the shortest end of the educational stick.

Jack Robinson knew all this. He knew that what hung in the balance as baseballs hurtled at him at ninety miles per hour was more than his personal success or that of the Dodgers and even more than how eighteen or nineteen million black people would feel as they went to bed that night. He had to know that as America tried out new postwar patterns of life, his performance as an athlete and as a man would be a shaping and seminal national experience. Occasionally the world gets to watch men consciously submerge themselves and their own personal desires under the fierce lash of a discipline born out of an understanding that they are required to serve something far greater than personal destiny. Few are given such opportunities, fewer still recognize them, and only a handful still have the courage, discipline, and skill to submerge self, rise to the challenge, and perform superbly. In eighteenth-century America a rich farmer named Washington and in twentieth-century Africa a black lawyer named Mandela both did it. And each changed the course of history.

Some might think that the analogy to Washington and Mandela is extreme. But, consider what Jack Robinson achieved: Day after day his dignified carriage and his brilliant play bored into the souls of virtually every American male and millions of white minds about who blacks were and what we might be able to accomplish.

And he made almost every black person in America better and bigger. He began—in a massive and nationwide way—to put pride inside our souls where shame had been. And he began to give millions of us a sense that things no longer needed to be as they had always been.

We do not know how many formerly fearful people came forward to join the NAACP because of their pride in Jack Roosevelt Robinson. We do not know how many people were emboldened to sign up for the lawsuits that finally found their way to the Supreme Court as *Brown v. Board of Education* seven years after he began to play. And we do not know how many more people were given the courage to demonstrate in Montgomery and Oklahoma City and in Greensboro later on because of what he did. But we do know how much shame and hurt we blacks would have felt if he had gone out and gotten drunk, participated in bar fights, and instigated on-field brawls in that fateful year of 1947. We've seen plenty of black *and* white athletes behave that way as the years have gone by. And we surely know the contempt so many whites would have felt for him and, by implication, the rest of us had he failed in any of those ways.

"Not ready for American life" would have been the general verdict rendered on us and, "Not ready for American life," many of us would have answered silently, deep in our souls, as we anguished in our public humiliation. All progress would not have stopped, obviously, had Jack let us down. It would simply have slowed significantly. But he did not let us down. He lifted us up. He carried the whole nation on his broad black shoulders. He marched through both the muck of white racism and the pain of culturally shriveled black spirits. When he got through, he had left all of us with far more room to grow than we had ever had before he began.

Only Rachel and her children can ever guess what this great human being's enormous gift to his nation cost him, and them. But we need not guess about the enormity of our debt of gratitude to all of them. We are a better people and a better nation for what he did and for the ways in which they helped him. It is a debt that can be paid only by remembering, understanding, and loving.

Roger Wilkins

P R E F A C E

Several years ago, as the fiftieth anniversary of Jackie Robinson's breaking the color barrier in baseball loomed, I felt inspired to contribute to the portrait that was to be drawn of him. This book is the result of these inner urgings to recount some of the experiences we shared during our thirty-two years together. As I undertook the project I felt most fortunate to enter the present stage of my life with a vigorous spirit, vital involvements, and a mind and soul filled with great and sometimes painful memories—memories that bring joy, laughter, and occasionally tears.

Jack's life spanned some of the most turbulent years in America's history. During this time we and many others successfully fought battle after battle, but I'm painfully aware that despite the progress, challenges and threats remain. I passionately hope that, by documenting Jack's triumphant struggle to cope with both the opportunities and the obstacles, all people, especially young people, will realize that they need not despair. The example of Jack's life shows that a fighting spirit and hard work can overcome great obstacles.

The story of Jack's baseball exploits has been told many times. Now, through photographs and my personal commentary, I seek to illuminate the forces that affected our public and private lives, and share the importance of our deep love and respect for each other and our families.

This book is my tribute to all fighters and believers who, like Jack, confronted injustice at an incalculable cost and yet carved out a clear direction for us to follow. Included in my salute is Branch Rickey, the man and all that he symbolized. This is also my first opportunity to publicly extol the accomplishments of my surviving adult children, Sharon and David, who lived through these complicated years and have remained resilient and hopeful. They have continued to pursue their dreams and have become professionals and strong and loving parents: Sharon, mother of Jesse Simms, and David, father to Susan Thomas, Howard Eaton, Rachel, Ayo, Li, and Faith Robinson. As a family we will forever remember and love Jackie, Jr., who tragically perished in the social wars of our times. We treasure his adult child, Sonya Pankey, and her daughter, Sherita, who represent his branch of the family with pride and great dignity. Finally, my optimism is sustained and inspired by the work of the Jackie Robinson Foundation, whose board, staff, supporters, and Jackie Robinson Scholars have given life to this legacy and carried Jack's spirit forward. I especially wish to acknowledge the extraordinary contribution of N.Y.U. Professor Michael Lutzker and his graduate students, who established the Foundation's award-winning archival collection from which many of the photographs and references in this book are drawn; it forms an integral part of the Foundation's educational mission.

For their help in the production of this work I am deeply grateful to Paul Gottlieb, Publisher of Harry N. Abrams; Owen Laster, my agent, who enthusiastically assisted me in launching this book; my collaborator Lee Daniels, who encouraged me to write and brought his professional skill and guidance to the work; Sharon AvRutick, my editor, who from our very first meeting generously supported the project, and who has helped me immeasurably in enhancing the presentation; designer Ray Hooper, who gave our book its style; and also John Crowley, my photo editor, who helped with the difficult task of selection from an abundant collection. I'm also indebted to my talented research assistants, Kathy Robinson (daughter of Mack Robinson), Patricia Hammock, and Sarah Elizabeth Jones, who delved into archival material, and in general joined in the spirit of our work together with the determination to absorb and preserve history.

I would also like to acknowledge the following organizations and people: Joe Black, Hank Aaron, Jackie Robinson Foundation, John Muir High School, Los Angeles Dodgers, Inc., National Baseball Hall of Fame and Museum, Inc., Pasadena City College, Pasadena Historical Museum, *Pasadena Star News*, Schomberg Center for Research in Black Culture, Bill Schumann, Scotts United Methodist Church, Claire Smith, Society for American Baseball Research (S.A.B.R.), *The Sporting News*, Jules Tygiel, and the University of California at Los Angeles.

Preparing this book and revisiting the decades of memories it encompasses has reaffirmed for me the indisputable truth that our destinies as people are inextricably linked.

Mallie Robinson

RICH BEGINNINGS

allie McGriff Robinson, Jack's
mother, was an extraordinary woman, spiritually deep, resourceful, and indomitable.
And she was a voluble storyteller, as I discovered in the early 1940s when I spent many
an hour sitting on the front porch of her home in Pasadena listening to stories about her
family. In 1920 her husband, Jerry, had abandoned her and their five children, Edgar,
Frank, Mack, Willa Mae, and Jack, to the bitter poverty of sharecropping on the Jim
Sasser farm in Cairo, Georgia. Driven by the hopeless circumstances in which they lived,
and Sasser, who furiously blamed Mallie for Jerry's disappearance, she packed up the
children and their belongings and boarded the train, the "Freedom Train" as she always
called it, for California.

*A portrait of Mallie Robinson
(seated) and her children (left to right):
Mack, Jack, Edgar, Willa Mae,
and Frank.*

Her Uncle Burton, who lived in Pasadena and had urged her to leave Georgia,
welcomed them into his already large household. Soon his quarters proved to be too
crowded; anyway, Mallie wanted more. She wanted a house for her family, a real home,
and she got it, buying a four-bedroom cottage at 121 Pepper Street.

This was a white neighborhood, closed to black people by restrictive covenants, or
so its residents thought. But Mallie bought it from a Negro man who had acquired it by
using a light-complexioned relative to front for him. We don't quite know how she
managed, on a domestic's salary, to become the owner of this house with its big backyard, front lawn, and flower beds, but that she did was characteristic of her. The way
Mallie assessed things was simple: "Is this the environment I want for my kids and myself?
Can we flourish here?"

I think a lot of her determination came from her religious beliefs. She just felt the
Lord was watching over her and He would see to it that she got what she needed. She
quietly sang His praises as she moved from task to task. It didn't matter to her that the
neighbors petitioned and threatened to burn down the house. She didn't feel she needed
approval to make the move. She felt she had a right to be there. They all did.

When Jack was about eight years old, he was out sweeping the sidewalk in front of
the house one day when the little white girl across the street began to yell "Nigger! Nigger! Nigger!" at him. Jack retaliated by calling her a "cracker." This brought her father
storming out of the house, and he started to throw rocks at Jack. Well, Jack picked up
the rocks and threw them right back until the man's wife finally pulled him inside. Jack

ABOVE: *As Mallie watches from the porch of the house on Pepper Street in 1944 or '45, a grown-up Jackie Robinson plays ball with his nephew Teddy, Willa Mae's son.*
BELOW: *Jack's class at Washington Junior High School, 1935.*

learned early on to fight back, because Mallie, a pioneer who had escaped from the South, now refused to accept abuse in the North. She wasn't well educated in a formal sense, but she had the vision and courage to take actions of heroic dimensions. Jack always said he thought of her as "working magic."

The Mallie Robinson family was a poor family, but they were rich in values and strengths that helped them adapt, adjust, and overcome obstacles. Although Mallie literally moved away from her support structure in the South, she created a new base and somehow began to foster positive identity, self-esteem, and an intense feeling of entitlement, especially in Jack, her youngest.

The Pepper Street Gang

Occasionally, Jack would reminisce about the mischievous escapades of the "Pepper Street Gang," the multiracial "outcasts" of his neighborhood. His gang was more like the Little Rascals than the antisocial juvenile marauders known as gangs today. One of his friends, called "Little Jack" Gordon, was "Big Jack"'s companion and informal protector most of his adult life. If you were a black, Hispanic, or Asian youngster in the Pasadena of the 1920s and 1930s you were allowed in the local YMCA only one day a week. The same rule was enforced at the city's big Brookside Park, which had an enticing swimming pool. So these boys had to devise their own recreation and in doing so, seemed to act out the frustrations that stemmed from the rejection they felt. They would swoop by fruit carts and steal oranges, apples, and whatever else they could grab. More enterprisingly, they would hang out in the rough of the golf course and steal the balls hit off the course, wash them, and then take them to the clubhouse to sell. They snitched what they could from the local stores. And they were rowdy. Once, the sheriff took them to jail at gunpoint for swimming in the reservoir. They did enough of these things in a public-enough way that they got well acquainted with Captain Morgan, the head of the police youth division.

Fortunately, their escapades also brought them to the attention of two other men. One was Carl Anderson, a mechanic who had several talks with Jack, telling him in man-to-man fashion that gang behavior wasn't for him. The other was Reverend Karl Downs, the new pastor of Pasadena's Scotts Methodist Church, who was to become a major influence in Jack's life.

The Blessing of Karl Downs

Reverend Karl Downs at home in the early 1940s with his wife, Marian, and their daughter, Karleen.

The most important men in Jack's life were his brothers, Frank, Edgar, and Mack, until Karl Downs came to Scotts Methodist Church. Jack always said he thought of Karl as stubborn and courageous because, against the opposition of the church elders, he organized clubs and teams to attract youngsters and bring them into the church. He knew they needed to develop a sense of belonging and the sense of responsibility that comes with it. Karl had the unique ability to join in their games and outings like a big brother, but he never lost his focus on religious and ethical teachings or his standing as their spiritual adviser. He would invite them to his home, an invitation that included giving them full access to his refrigerator. To this group of always-hungry young men, who were rarely welcomed into other people's homes, there was nothing more meaningful; it was a sign of trust and intimacy.

Jack and Karl became especially close friends. Jack said Karl's intervention—he called it a "rescue"—changed the course of his life. His father, Jerry, had simply disappeared—and Jack never expressed any interest in him—but he did seem to gravitate toward good men like Karl Downs. And the religious beliefs that Karl helped stimulate in him would strengthen his ability to cope with all the challenges he would face in his life. Like Mallie, Jack felt God's presence in the most personal way. To a fatherless boy, Karl offered not only a spiritual awakening but also a sense of direction; for instance, Jack taught in the Sunday School program as his way of giving back. And, as confidant and companion, Karl found ways of helping Jack well past his adolescent years, including getting him a short-term coaching position in Austin, Texas, one of Jack's first jobs after leaving UCLA.

Karl blessed our marriage and lived to celebrate the birth of Jackie, Jr., in 1946. We were inconsolable when he died suddenly on February 26, 1948. The loss was the more wrenching for us because we were then embarking on a new phase of our life and passionately wanted him to share it with us.

Roots of a Relationship

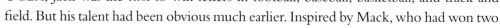

U C L A

ne of the greatest athletes in the history of UCLA, Jack was the first to win letters in football, baseball, basketball, and track and field. But his talent had been obvious much earlier. Inspired by Mack, who had won two

Jack's brother Mack was a superb athlete.

sprinting medals at the 1936 Olympics in Berlin, and urged on by brother Frank, his biggest fan, Jack had been a four-letterman at John Muir Technical High School. That drew the interest of several colleges with top sports programs, but at first Jack chose to go to Pasadena Junior College (PJC), a two-year school, so that he could stay home and be able to help Mallie. At PJC Jack starred in football, track, and baseball, the last two in the same season. He was gleeful the day he broke brother Mack's broad-jump record at 25 feet, ½ inch, and then managed to change uniforms and star in a baseball game. In 1938, he led Pasadena to the Junior College Championship and was named the Most Valuable Junior College Player in Southern California. His spirited play made him a team leader and an outstanding prospect for college teams.

Shortly after Jack entered UCLA in 1939, Frank was killed in a motorcycle accident. Jack was devastated; of his brothers, he felt closest to Frank. The tragedy made him even more committed to excelling in sports as his special tribute to a lost brother.

Jack was a well-known campus hero by the time I entered UCLA in the fall of 1940. He and his teammates Woody Strode and Kenny Washington made UCLA's black students—few in number, of course—extremely proud of our school and our race. Like most black students, including Jack, I lived at home and commuted to the campus (I drove an old, beat-up Ford V-8), which created a sense of isolation from campus life. Our after-school jobs off-campus intensified this feeling. Rooting for the sports teams was one important connection to the university. Another was gathering between classes in Kerckhoff Hall, the student union, a splendid stone building in the center of UCLA's campus. The black athletes like Woody, Kenny, and Jack were a big part of what drew us to that location. Jack was sought after by many of the women on campus, but he later

ABOVE: *In 1936 Mack Robinson (left) won the silver medal in the 200-meter dash at the Olympic Games in Berlin. Jesse Owens (right) won the gold medal and set a new world record with a time of twenty-one seconds flat. They are shown here in a qualifying event, also finishing first and second.* LEFT: *This photograph of Jack's brother Frank, his biggest fan, was taken shortly before Frank's tragic death in 1939.* RIGHT: *Willa Mae Robinson, Jack's sister, with her friend John. She was a second mother to Jack, making it possible for Mallie to go to work and leave baby Jack well cared for.*

Mallie talking with her sons Mack and Jack in their living room. Notice my picture in the background.

told me that he was wary of involvement with them because they were attracted to him as an athlete without knowing what he was like as a person.

When we met, I was immediately drawn to him. He was very impressive—a handsome, proud, and serious man with a warm smile and a pigeon-toed walk. And he felt drawn to me as well, but we both were shy and intent on reaching the goals we had set for ourselves. For me, getting a degree was my highest priority. I would let nothing interfere with it. Still, our relationship blossomed. We casually met in the parking lot and other public places until I invited him home to meet my family. My mother saw the best in him, my father was jealous, and my brothers were in awe.

ABOVE: *Jack, UCLA's first four-letter man, established outstanding records in football, baseball, track, and basketball. On June 10, 1984, he was inducted into the UCLA Sports Hall of Fame.* LEFT: *Teaming up with Kenny Washington to create an All-American backfield, a legendary collegiate pairing.*

LEFT: *Jack led the Pacific Coast Conference in scoring twice during his college basketball career.*
RIGHT: *While attending Pasadena Junior College, Jack held the national junior college broad jump record, and later, in 1940, he won the NCAA broad jump title at 25 feet, 6½ inches.*

Stepping Out

On our first formal date, Jack invited me to attend a Bruin football dinner at the Biltmore Hotel in Los Angeles. I was eighteen years old and had never been a guest in a hotel, which added to the excitement I felt at the thought of entering the lobby on Jack's arm. I managed to keep my anxiety in check by focusing on what to wear and how to look older. I went to the May Company basement store and bought my first black dress and a fur-trimmed hat, and I borrowed my grandmother's old broadtail fur coat to top off my outfit.

But correct dress was not enough. My anxiety had a lot to do with knowing about the Northern-style bigotry so common in Los Angeles; unlike the South, incidents of discrimination were often unexpected and inexplicable—you never knew when they would happen. As a child growing up on the west side of Los Angeles, my friends and I were regularly directed straight from the lobby of our neighborhood movie house to the balcony. We never protested or informed our parents. We didn't understand the significance of the action being taken against us. To me the Biltmore Hotel represented not just glitz and glamour, but the possibility that we wouldn't be welcomed. I had to be mentally prepared.

Everything went well. Jack flirted with me, and we danced the fox-trot, in keeping with the occasion, although the lindy-hop was more my style and would have allowed me to express my joy in dance.

LEFT: *The smile that attracts . . . me.*
BELOW: *Kerckhoff Hall, the student union, is a beautiful stone building on the UCLA campus where black students often gathered. Most notably, it's the place where Jack's friend Ray Bartlett introduced us.*

ABOVE: *A Bruin dinner held at the Biltmore Hotel in Los Angeles was the occasion of our first date. I dressed in black to look older.*
RIGHT: *After he left UCLA Jack was hired to play football for the semipro Honolulu Bears. Their first exhibition game was in Pearl Harbor. Jack left Honolulu on December 5, just before the December 7 bombing. He's shown here with his friend Ray Bartlett (far left) as they dock in Honolulu to begin the season.*

 *The Army*

T H E W A R A T H O M E

*I*t was early 1942 when Jack got his draft notice. The family gathered at Mallie's house in Pasadena to discuss what he should do. Actually, it was pretty clear what his choice would be.

Jack had spent the fall in Honolulu playing semipro football with the Honolulu Bears and had left Pearl Harbor on December 5, just two days before the Japanese attack devastated the military base. He was on board the *Lurline*, sailing home, when Congress formally declared war. Jack fully shared the outrage that most of America felt about the attack. At that time he was a patriotic man and felt that he, as much as any American, owed it to the country to fight for freedom. So, after talking it over, he decided not to seek a deferment by claiming family hardship.

Despite the fact that discrimination was still widespread and the military itself was rigidly segregated, Jack, like many black men, joined the armed forces with high expectations. President Franklin Roosevelt had given his historic "Four Freedoms" speech outlining what America was fighting to defend, and had issued the first Fair Employment order prohibiting discrimination in wartime jobs. Jack and his buddy from Pasadena, Roscoe DeVore, were inducted into the United States Army on April 3, 1942, in a hopeful mood.

The United States armed forces were segregated until 1948, when President Harry Truman ordered that the armed forces and federal workplaces be integrated.

I was, at best, ambivalent. I would soon have three men I loved in the military: Jack; my older brother, Chuck, who would become a Tuskegee airman (he would be shot down over Yugoslavia late in the war and would spend months in a prisoner-of-war camp); and my younger brother, Raymond, who would serve in the Pacific. But enough had already happened in my family's history of military service for me to consider war a personal, potent, and destructive force: My father had been gassed in France in World War I and suffered a forty percent disability following the war.

Meanwhile, I was already involved in the war effort in my own way. I trained and took a lucrative job as a riveter on the night shift at Lockheed Aircraft. For a year, I worked nights, went to UCLA at dawn, and after changing clothes in the parking lot, proceeded to class. I spent my last three years of college at U.C. San Francisco School of Nursing studying to be a registered nurse. Student nurses staffed the hospital wards for full eight-hour shifts and took a full course load as well. My own participation helped me accept Jack's enlistment and the prolonged absences.

Although Jack had been exposed to bigotry in the North, nothing had prepared him for the intensity of his reaction to the discrimination of the army bases in the South. Because he refused to passively accept the injustices inflicted on black soldiers, his period of service from 1942 until his court-martial and honorable discharge in 1944 was filled with challenges and trouble.

The earliest challenges were simple and even humorous. Assigned to the cavalry, he was never comfortable handling a rifle, and was awkward on a horse. He wrote home giving funny descriptions of his efforts to master them both.

While posted first to Fort Riley, Kansas, Jack found the most emotionally wrenching aspect of army life was attempting to gain the most basic accommodations for black men. For instance, in a large post exchange (PX), a store on the base that sells merchandise and services to military personnel and authorized civilians, black soldiers were allotted half the seats they needed and stood, angry yet compliant, in long lines staring at white soldiers sitting in comfort with seats to spare. The inadequate accommodations and the army's refusal to process his application for Officers' Candidate School (OCS) were representative of the pervasive humiliating environment that undercut the morale of the men. Jack could never remain silent or passive in the face of injustice, and his defiance of the policies did lead to some positive results. Space for black soldiers in the PX was increased, and the army hierarchy was alerted to the need for a morale officer. Jack became that officer.

Private Robinson in his cavalry uniform.

Joe Louis, the world heavyweight champ, who enlisted in the army and enhanced the war effort, was also the literal symbol of black Americans' fight for freedom. His arrival at Fort Riley brought much-needed power to the black soldiers and gave Jack an opportunity to form an alliance and work with his longtime hero. Louis used his Washington contacts to rally support for the black soldiers' cause, forcing the army to open the door for black OCS candidates to prepare them for promotion. Jack became a second lieutenant on January 28, 1943. Second Lieutenant Jackie Robinson enjoyed more influence with certain superiors, but not for long. He was considered a troublemaker, and soon found himself at war at home.

RIGHT: *Sergeant Raymond Isum, my younger brother. All the men in my family served in a U.S. war. Raymond served in New Guinea, the Philippines, and Tokyo in 1942–45. He was wounded, as were the others, and received the Purple Heart.*

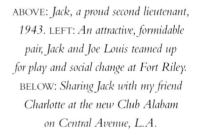

ABOVE: *Jack, a proud second lieutenant, 1943.* LEFT: *An attractive, formidable pair, Jack and Joe Louis teamed up for play and social change at Fort Riley.* BELOW: *Sharing Jack with my friend Charlotte at the new Club Alabam on Central Avenue, L.A.*

It was at this dance, while Jack was on
furlough in San Francisco, that we
announced our engagement.

7

The Court~Martial

As I have said, it didn't matter that the United States of America was fighting a two-front war against powerful enemies—the military was determined to continue its Jim Crow treatment of black soldiers and sailors. After receiving his commission as a second lieutenant, Jack was transferred to Camp Hood, Texas, and was fortunate to come under the command of Colonel R. L. Bates, a proponent of fairness who struggled within an unjust system.

Jack had bone chips in his ankle from his football days, and on July 6, 1944, had gone to the base hospital to have them examined. Catching the bus on the post back to the barracks, he ran into the wife of one of his brother lieutenants, and they sat together, talking. The woman was African-American, but light complexioned. The white bus driver became incensed at a black second lieutenant talking with a woman he thought was white. He stopped the bus and ordered Jack to move to the rear. Jack, knowing that army regulations had recently been issued that barred racial discrimination on any vehicle operating on an army post, refused. The bus driver started shouting at him, and Jack, being Jack, shouted right back and said he was not budging. Well, when the bus got to the last stop on the post, the driver rushed off and returned with his dispatcher and other drivers, pointing at Jack and shouting, "There's the nigger that's been causing trouble!"

A military police jeep pulled up almost immediately, and the two military policemen very politely asked Jack to come with them to M.P. headquarters. It soon became clear to him that he was being accused of being drunk and disorderly, so he immediately took a blood test to disprove that. At that moment, it didn't matter that he had not had a drink in his life.

Although the charges were unsubstantiated, the court-martial went ahead, and Jack became very concerned that he was all alone facing a charge that could put him in the stockade on an army base fraught with racial tension. He conferred with Colonel Bates, who had long been sympathetic to the plight of the black soldier, but Jack felt that he needed outside guidance as well. He felt so threatened that he wrote to the NAACP asking for "advice and counsel."

Assistant Special Counsel Edward Dudley wrote back, "Please be advised that we will be unable to furnish you with an attorney in the event that you are court-martialed. However, if following the court-martial you feel that you have received an unfair sentence, kindly communicate with us at your earliest convenience, enclosing a copy of the court record, and we will be very happy to review same in order to determine whether we can make representations on your behalf before the Judge Advocate General's Board of Review, in Washington, D.C."

Also, a letter signed "anonymous" and dated July 20, 1944, was sent presumably from fellow officers to the NAACP alerting them that a conspiracy was forming to "railroad" Jack by having witnesses tell lies to the panel. The final sentence of this letter states, "This incident is only one of many which have seen Negro officers and enlisted men intimidated and mistreated in Camp Hood and surrounding towns."

Archival records show that the army itself was very concerned about the case, too. As the transcript of a telephone conversation between Jack's commanding officer and the chief of staff states, "This is a very serious case and it is full of dynamite. It requires very delicate handling."

On August 2, 1944, after hours of testimony from the prosecution led by Captains Gerald Bear and Peelor Wigginton, from witnesses clearly lacking in credibility, Jack's lawyer, Lieutenant William Cline, summed up by saying that this was not a case "involving any violation of the Articles of War . . . but simply a situation in which a few individuals sought to vent their bigotry on a Negro they considered 'uppity.' " Jack was acquitted that same day.

Realizing that the court-martial had caused him to miss going overseas with Bates' outfit, Jack was disgusted and wanted out. He deliberately violated military protocol by writing a letter directly to the Adjutant General's office in Washington about his case. He figured this would get results quickly, and it did. On November 28, 1944, using the fact that Jack had bone chips in his ankle, the army gave him an honorable discharge.

8

The Negro Leagues

THE OPEN DOOR

When Jack joined the Kansas City Monarchs for spring training in 1945 and entered the world of the Negro Leagues, black baseball had never been better. Its style, which emphasized speed and daring, was far more exciting than the deliberate, slow approach of the major leagues. Who said so? The fans—in 1942 three million people watched the Negro Leaguers play. While major-league attendance declined during the war years, the Negro League teams played to packed stadiums and enjoyed greater financial success than at any time in their history.

*Jack and his
Kansas City Monarch teammates.*

True, major-league baseball had lost such players as Ted Williams, Joe DiMaggio, and Hank Greenberg to the military. But the Negro teams had lost stars, too. There was something in the play and players of the Negro Leagues that captured the essence of black life in America—the continuing playing of the game with skill and grace and enjoyment, despite the obstacles. That was the standard Satchel Paige and Buck Leonard and Josh Gibson and other Negro League stars set.

And yet, it became clear in hindsight that Jack's joining the Negro Leagues was actually the beginning of the end for black baseball.

Jack's becoming a Negro Leaguer was really the result of his grabbing at a lifeline. About to get out of the army, he was a man without a college degree and without marketable skills. He was desperate to get a job, to help support Mallie, and to marry me. One day while waiting for his discharge papers to come through, he started throwing a

Top Row

BLANCO CHATAING   ROY CAMPANELLA   MARVIN BARKER   BILL ANDERSON   QUINCY TROUPPE
GEORGE JEFFERSON   PARNELL WOODS   ROY WELMAKER   BUCK LEONARD,   BOTTOM ROW
JACKIE ROBINSON   EUGENE BENSON   FELTON SNOW   VERDEL MATHIS   SAM JETHROE   TRAINER
AMERICAN ALL STARS   MGR.   CARACAS, VENEZUELA

1945

ABOVE: *Frequently, at the end of a season, all-star teams were organized to barnstorm and add to the season's salary. Shown here are the American All-Stars on a trip in Venezuela, 1945. Jack is the first person in the front row and Campy is second from the left in the back.* OPPOSITE: *Jack visits with Satchel Paige, the great Monarch pitcher.*

ball around with another black GI who had played for the Monarchs. They struck up a conversation, and the fellow told him that the Monarchs were looking for players. Jack wrote to the organization and they invited him for a tryout. During spring training he was signed at a salary of $400 a month, and when he got a spot on the team, he felt he had hit paydirt.

But Jack quickly came to hate life in the Negro Leagues. Oh, the camaraderie among the players was wonderful. He always had fond memories of that. But still, in his autobiography, *I Never Had It Made*, published in October 1972, he called it "a pretty miserable way to make a buck." Travel schedules were "unbelievably hectic" and tiring, and, of course, there were very few places along the road where they could sit down to a decent meal or check into a decent motel. The Negro Leaguers endured great deprivation, and Jack felt the daily indignities and disrespect particularly keenly.

So, when Branch Rickey sent a scout to approach him, Jack was ready to listen to anything that would get him out of the Negro Leagues.

Rickey~Robinson

A D A R I N G P A I R

*I*n my mind, Branch Rickey and Jackie Robinson will be forever linked and thought of as a "daring pair." For me the wonder of it all is that these two men, who came from distinctly different backgrounds and positions in life, together embarked on an extraordinary journey—and reached their goal.

Branch Rickey, described by Arthur Mann, one of his biographers, as a visionary with "pioneering ideas . . . a family man with high regard for the truth, and a stubborn person who refused compromise," took over as general manager of the Brooklyn Dodgers in 1942, at the age of sixty-one. Rickey had been hired because he was known as a brilliant baseball man. He had been with the St. Louis Cardinals for twenty-five years, rising to vice president and business manager. While there, Rickey had organized one of baseball's great innovations, the farm system, which enabled the Cards to compete with richer clubs by developing their own players. Rickey was a man open to the need for change, unlike many baseball owners and general managers who were notorious for resisting it. Most of all, Rickey was a fierce competitor who was determined to win. The O'Malley family had hired him to make the Dodgers a championship team, and he was often quoted as saying he wanted the kind of players who would "help me win a pennant in Brooklyn." He rarely, if ever, spoke publicly about his interest in changing the racial character of baseball. But it is known that he had been moved by earlier experiences, while coaching at Ohio Wesleyan, with a black athlete on his team who suffered racial attacks in Rickey's presence. Rickey did not discuss his racial beliefs, but his social concerns seemed implicit in his actions.

In August 1945, he sent his competent scout Clyde Sukeforth to Chicago's Comiskey Park, where the Monarchs were playing. Sukeforth's job was to evaluate Jackie Robinson, whose name had surfaced repeatedly in scouting reports. Clyde, a soft-spoken man with reassuring sincerity, was the perfect man to represent Rickey. Jack had become cynical about the intentions of white owners after an April 16 "tryout" with the Boston Red Sox. *The Pittsburgh Courier*'s crusading sportswriter Wendell Smith had arranged it for Jack, Sam Jethroe of the Cleveland Buckeyes, and Marvin Williams of the Philadelphia Stars—all leading hitters in the Negro Leagues. Neither the manager nor any players showed up at Fenway Park that day, and it turned out to be a humiliating charade for both Wendell and Jack. But Clyde seemed worth following.

So on August 28, 1945, Jack flew to New York for a meeting with Branch Rickey—the meeting at which he would be hired. This was the occasion of the much-reported role-playing session in which Rickey subjected Jack to every form of racial attack he could imagine to test his strengths and prepare him for the ordeals sure to come. The two men also arrived at an important agreement: Jack promised that regard-less of the provocation he would not retaliate in any way. Although the session aroused in Jack what he described as a "weird mixture of emotions" he was impressed by Rickey's strength and apparent sincerity—impressed enough to accept the proposed opportunity.

One of the first questions Rickey had asked Jack was about us: "You got a girl?" Jack told him of our engagement. Rickey smiled and said, "You know you have a girl. When we get through today you may want to call her up because there are times when a man needs a woman by his side."

Following the meeting in New York, Jack called me in California, jubilant and yet

1945: The historic meeting of J.R. and Branch Rickey—the legendary coming together of the daring pair.

secretive, to say he had an unheard-of chance to try out for the major leagues. I could only respond to the excitement in his voice, as I couldn't envision what the opportunity might be. Frankly, I just hoped it meant he had a job at last, since we had been engaged for five years, and were waiting for the right moment to get married. I had just graduated in June (with the Florence Nightingale Award for clinical excellence) and was eager to get on with my life.

Rickey kept in close touch with us throughout the next two years and, in 1947, after Jack joined the team in Brooklyn, would periodically invite us to meet privately with him in his hotel suite. I came to view these visits as quiet strategy sessions, opportunities to discuss developments and anticipate complications in a setting where we didn't have to worry about being interrupted or misinterpreted. Jack and Rickey cemented the life-long trust and respect they felt for each other in those sessions, and I sat quietly and watched them work with pride and satisfaction.

I believe they got along so well because temperamentally they were well matched; Rickey had the very traits that he sought in Jack. Both were religious. Both had an unshakable integrity, and both possessed a hard-headed determination to compete at their best. There was no doubt about Rickey's business objectives, but equally clear to us was his intense commitment to making integration work, which he tended to underplay in public. He and Jack were unequal in power and influence to be sure, but they were always interdependent in this social experiment. Neither could succeed without the other.

Jack was neither docile nor passive—except when they were talking salary. When that time arrived, Branch Rickey was like every other baseball businessman; in fact, he was reported to be the worst. Baseball in the forties allowed players no salary negotiations—period. Jack accepted what was offered. He had no illusions about Rickey's business interests and never believed his motives to be simply altruistic. In fact, his vested interest in creating a winning team was reassuring to us. We could also see and appreciate Rickey's vision, meticulous planning, and sensitive anticipation of our needs as signs of an unwavering commitment to the social ideal. He was accessible, though Jack didn't tend to call him, and willing to take charge when trouble surfaced. He gave us, young adults in our twenties, confidence, and we learned to mobilize our own strengths independently.

For me, Branch Rickey became a familiar source of comfort. I could count on him. I admired him and thought that he was so often caricatured by the press that the substance of the man was lost. When he crouched down by first base in spring training waving his hat and shouting at Jack, "Be daring, be daring," my spirit embraced them both with pride.

ABOVE: *As a child, I absorbed my family's belief in FDR's extraordinary powers of leadership. My first job was sponsored by the National Youth Administration. His death, just prior to my college graduation, was a blow to my sense of security.*
LEFT: *Nurse Rachel Isum, in that distinctive U.C. nursing cap.* BELOW: *My roommate Janice Lewis (second from right) and I—along with other friends— graduate from the University of California, June 1945.*

OPPOSITE: *Brooklyn Dodgers president Branch Rickey, the pioneer who integrated baseball, warned Jack of trials to come. He was shrewd in business and thoughtful in personal relationships.*

10

Wed at Last

*Married on February 10, 1946, at
the Independent Church, Los Angeles.
Our day had finally come.*

In 1941 Jack and I had become formally engaged, with a ring and the announcement to family and friends. It was my sophomore year at UCLA, and within months Jack was shipped off to the army base at Fort Riley, Kansas. The war had created tension and uncertainty in our lives, as in the lives of millions of others, and the commitment that our engagement implied gave us a heady feeling of attachment and security in our love. The 1941 death of my father, for whom I had great respect and love, had left me grief stricken. I had been his guardian angel, as watchful and protective of him in his late life as if he were my vulnerable child. The deep respect and devotion I felt for Jack was reminiscent of this earlier love. The passion was new.

The war forced us to endure long, painful separations—it would be five years before our marriage on February 10, 1946. I was in the last three years of my nursing program in San Francisco, determined to graduate. Jack was hundreds of miles away in the middle of the country, able to get away for only short furloughs. It was a strained engagement, at times putting our relationship to the most severe test of loyalty and faith. But we remained steadfast despite temptations and the turmoil around us. In fact, I believe that having to struggle through these years helped us mature and prepare for our life together.

The arrangements for the wedding were largely determined by the dreams my mother, Zellee, had for her only daughter. She had eloped at a young age, and so she had missed having an elaborate ceremony. For my wedding, naturally, she wanted all the traditional elements: a wedding gown made of prewar ivory satin, a long train, a fetching veil, luscious bouquets of flowers, and just the right music. She prevailed upon us to select a large, old Negro church in West Los Angeles and organize a full complement of beautifully attired attendants. Fortunately, Jack was already fond of my mother, so together we happily indulged her fantasies—church, dress, flowers, and all. What was most important to us was to have Karl Downs, Jack's dear friend, unite us, and to be surrounded by our childhood friends, including several members of the Pepper Street Gang.

The wedding reception in my home on 36th Place fulfilled my most cherished expectations, except for a prank played on us by "Little Jack" Gordon and "the boys." They decided to hide our getaway car, and then denied having done it, holding us

RIGHT: *My friends Florence Nukes
(far left), Charlotte Robinson, and
Josephine Marshall (right), with my
cousin Flora Boswell (second from left).*
BELOW RIGHT: *Jack, surrounded by his
best men (left to right): Sidney
Heard, Pete McCullough, my brother
Chuck Williams, Buddy Devine,
and "Little Jack" Gordon.*

hostage with them until most of the guests were gone. But even this final bit of devil-try couldn't spoil a perfect day. Jack radiated happiness and pride. His mother, Mallie, and my brothers, Chuck and Raymond, completed our wedding party and formed the core of our new family.

That night, when we entered our hotel on Central Avenue, and finally closed the door on the outer world, all of my fears and doubts vanished. It was a precious moment filled with feelings of completeness.

We were thrilled to be married by Karl Downs.

ABOVE: *As we prepared to cut the wedding cake, a current of excitement passed through us. My bouquet is composed of a dozen white orchids.* LEFT: *The wedding reception. My grandmother Annetta Jones and Mallie Robinson are on the left, and Zellee Isum (my mother) and my brother Raymond are on the right.* OPPOSITE: *Alone at last.*

11

First Spring Training

D A Y T O N A   B E A C H

*Dressed in wedding finery, we board
a bus from Pensacola to Daytona Beach.
We had been bumped from two planes
earlier and still managed to smile.*

Two weeks after our marriage, in a festive, confident mood, we prepared to go south to Daytona Beach, Florida, for our first spring training. Jack would be training with the Montreal Royals, a triple-A team in the Brooklyn Dodgers farm system. The pathway to the major leagues . . . we hoped. Little did we know, as we said good-bye to Mallie Robinson at the airport, that for the next few weeks we would be engaged in a constant struggle against degradation. Dear Mallie had an inkling: She brought us a shoe box of fried chicken to take on the plane. Her experience of traveling in the South had taught her to be prepared, to be as self-sufficient as possible: "God bless the child who's got his own." I must admit to having had an unguarded faith in being American, although I did have some trepidation about entering the South for the first time. But dressed in my wedding finery and escorted by my strong, handsome, talented husband, I couldn't foresee the need for the odorous chicken as we parted from Mallie. I was focusing on my hope that whatever the circumstances, Jack would land a desperately needed job and win a place in the starting lineup.

We were particularly concerned about arriving in Daytona on time and ready for work. We were all too familiar with the racial stereotype widely believed by whites and too often acted out by blacks.

Our troubles began almost immediately upon entering the South. As our American Airlines flight approached the New Orleans airport, we were paged and told we were being removed from the plane, "bumped," as they called it, without explanation or recourse. We went into the terminal and challenged the decision. As Jack's voice began to rise in protest at the counter, I escaped to the ladies' room, only to be confronted with "White Women" and "Colored Women" signs. Shocked and indignant, I rushed into the white ladies' room with such speed and determination that I was stared at but not stopped. I re-emerged, my self-esteem momentarily restored, and joined Jack. It was clear that his appeal had failed. There were no more planes that day, so we proceeded to a seedy hotel, as directed.

That evening we sat on the side of the bed and pulled out Mallie's chicken. As we quietly ate, I could feel humiliation and a sense of powerlessness overpowering me. More importantly, I appreciated Mallie's wisdom as never before.

This early setback was merely a foreshadowing of trials to come. I think that is

when I began to sit up straighter and tighten the muscles in my waist. The next day, after two hours in the air, we were bumped again in Pensacola, Florida. Frustrated and angry, we made our way to the bus station. Although we were hungry, we agreed not to eat from the back-window takeout offered to blacks. We boarded the bus, automatically taking the first empty seats up front. Jack promptly went to sleep, and I sat watch. As white passengers boarded, the driver ordered us to the rear. I woke Jack, concerned about his reaction, especially given his fight in the army over this very same order. But, instead of challenging the driver, he docilely led me to the last seat in the rear. I followed in a mixed state of disbelief, relief, and pain. The relief did not last, and in the darkness I silently wept. My man had become the white South's "boy," in order to keep us safe.

However, even then I could see that we had the survivor's most crucial traits—resilience and indestructible hope. Surrounded by black people, we settled down on the back seat and took comfort in their closeness and courtesies. We finally arrived in Daytona and were met by Wendell Smith and Billy Rowe, a *Courier* photographer, whom Rickey had sent to accompany us throughout spring training. Billy later told me that Jack did explode with the pent-up anger inside him, only when I was out of view. I was already more focused on our next steps.

Exhausted, we went off to the home of Duff and Joe Harris, where Rickey had arranged for us to stay, apart from the team. We collapsed in each other's arms in our little room, which was to become a never-forgotten sanctuary.

Descending into the South meant coping with degradation.

Manager Clay Hopper and Branch Rickey, Jr. Hopper was able to overcome his Mississippi origins and managed Jack fairly. It's reported, though, that when Branch Rickey described a catch by Jack as a "superhuman play," Hopper responded, "Mr. Rickey, do you really think a nigger's a human being?"

The Pittsburgh Courier's Wendell Smith (left) and Billy Rowe (not shown) were our constant companions and supporters during the first spring training.

12

1946

SURVIVING THE CUT

The events surrounding Jack's entry into organized baseball in 1946 were well documented by our confidant Wendell Smith, the most influential advocate for the integration of baseball in this period; Sam Lacy, sports editor of *The Baltimore Afro-American*; and Joe Bostic, columnist for New York's *The People's Voice*—all major contributors to the process of change.

The forces arrayed against the social experiment led by Branch Rickey were many, and included the late Kenesaw Mountain Landis, major-league baseball's intransigent commissioner until 1944, and the smug and obstinate *The Sporting News*, whose negative predictions about Negro ballplayers gave unwilling owners cover to hide behind.

I mention these forces because Jack and I could feel the effects of the opposition even when the sources could not be clearly identified. We knew the powers opposed to baseball's desegregation were formidable and were bolstered by local laws and customs in Florida. Those laws served to personalize and legalize the attacks on us. Except for Wendell Smith; John Wright, a Negro pitcher who joined us; Branch Rickey, who was ever present; and Joe and Duff Harris, our gracious hosts, we were initially isolated in Daytona Beach and well aware of the threats and rumors of threats that swirled about Jack's presence on the team.

Even Branch Rickey's meticulous and thoughtful plan to house us with the Harrises, which put us in the middle of the political and intellectual stronghold of the Negro community, was the first capitulation to the prevailing forces in the South: It was done because the team's hotel refused to accommodate us. Although the Harris home was charming and eventually a haven filled with comfort and stimulation, the separate but equal accommodations could not disguise the fact that we were being excluded, labeled inferior, and tolerated only in the workplace.

I will be forever grateful to the Harrises. It was through them that we met and were inspired by one of my heroines, the proud and distinguished Mary McLeod Bethune, cofounder of historic Bethune-Cookman College, and adviser to presidents. We also met a rich array of influential community leaders, college faculty, and just interesting people who were sensitive to our changing needs for company, counseling, and solitude.

Compared to the adjacent towns, Daytona Beach stood out as a kind of political oasis. Its more liberal environment could be traced to organizations of Negro voters, its economic base in tourism, and baseball. We moved freely in downtown Daytona Beach,

Joe and Duff Harris created a home for us apart from the team. Our little room at the top of the staircase was our haven where we could share intimately and recuperate from the stresses of the day. Pictured here are Duff Harris and her dog.

and we were welcomed in the ballpark. However, nothing and no one could soften the blows from the bigotry we encountered in Jacksonville, Sanford, and Deland. Solely due to the presence of Jack and John Wright on the Royals' team roster, the team was locked out in Jacksonville and Deland and run out of the ballpark in Sanford. The ugly, contemptible environment created by these events took their toll on Jack, though his public statements denied the fact. He began to try too hard to win a permanent place on the team (rookies could be cut before the end of training), filled with anger generated by the situation. He was overswinging and having difficulty sleeping and concentrating. He went into a slump—that mysterious ailment that plagues even the best ballplayers from time to time—which at this particular point in Jack's life could have led to serious consequences. We were worried.

Our spirits soared at the end of this training period in Daytona Beach, for Jack regained his confidence, began hitting, and won a place on the team. The agricultural department at Bethune-Cookman sent over chicken and vegetables, which Duff and I used to cook a victory dinner. It was a communal victory for sure.

From the moment we were bumped from the American Airlines flights, my role had begun to unfold. It evolved and became more crucial over time. My most profound instinct as Jack's wife was to protect him—an impossible task. I could, however, be a consistent presence to witness and validate the realities, love him without reservation, share his thoughts and miseries, discover with him the humor in the ridiculous behavior against us, and, most of all, help maintain our fighting spirit. I knew our only chance to survive was to be ourselves.

13

Montreal

T H E   B E A U T I F U L   L A U N C H

rriving in Canada from the nightmare of Florida was like coming to the surface after being submerged in deep water.

Montreal was a beautiful international city completely unknown to us, and, as it turned out, it was the ideal place to launch Jack's career.

My first intimate encounter with the city came when I went apartment hunting. I selected a location from the Royals's list of available apartments, and went to an attached home on DeGaspé Street, in a French-Canadian neighborhood, and knocked on the door. The woman who opened it set the tone for our entire stay. She said "Welcome!" in English, and meant it. The baggage one carries in one's psyche can be intrusive in new experiences. Given the pervasive housing discrimination in the States, I had anticipated an unpleasant meeting.

As it turned out, the lady invited me in and prepared tea, and we chatted briefly. Our conversation went so well that I accepted the lovely apartment without looking further, and she offered to leave her linens, china, and crystal for our use. I felt that finding this temporary home effortlessly was a good omen, and we moved in.

ABOVE: *On October 23, 1945, Jack signed with the Montreal Royals. Branch Rickey, Jr., stands at the left, and Royals President Hector Racine (seated, left) and Vice President Romeo Gauvreau (right) look on.*
OPPOSITE: *Jack with John Wright in Montreal, important companions in the earliest days. Wright was sent down to Three Rivers in 1946 and returned to the Homestead Grays the next year.*

Not in my most wildly orchestrated fantasies could I have hoped for an opening day such as the one on April 18, 1946, in Roosevelt Stadium, Jersey City. When Montreal played the Jersey City Giants, there were bands, a sold-out crowd, and festivities that seemed to accompany the excitement I was feeling. The very air was charged on this historic occasion. Jackie Robinson was to be the first black athlete to play in organized baseball. I wandered through the aisles, too nervous to be seated at first. In his second turn at bat, Jack hit a three-run homer, and I sat down, nervous no more—our team and Jack were off to an auspicious start. From that point on, he proceeded to display his entire repertoire. He had four hits, two stolen bases, drove in three runs, bunted safely, and scored twice on balks by pitchers he rattled. *The Pittsburgh Courier* summed the feat up in a raving headline "Jackie Stole the Show."

The good will in our neighborhood in Montreal was reflected and magnified in Delormier Downs, the ballpark where Jack played with great distinction. We were buoyed by our other good news: I was pregnant. When I was certain of my pregnancy

and ready to share the news, I couldn't wait for Jack to return home from a road trip with the team to tell him. I wrote to him, and his tender response made my heart leap. On June 5, 1946, he began his letter with "My Dearest Darling, I just received your letter and I was so happy I nearly cried. . . . We will have loads of fun with Jr. . . . and don't worry. I'll give Jr. something to read about later in his life." He anticipated and obviously hoped for a Junior before we knew the gender of our unborn child.

Jack and I shared a longing for a family, in part because our families had always been at the center of our existence, and the news came at a time when we were beginning to have a glimpse of the future. The fans, black and white, and the rumblings about the progress Jack was making toward the major leagues had begun to convey to us the importance of our mission. We were beginning to understand that this was more than just a job opportunity.

Anticipating the birth of Jackie, Jr., gave us an added incentive to succeed. Our families in California were ecstatic, and our French-speaking neighbors responded to my condition like extended family. They kept a watchful eye on me, children running to meet me and carry packages, women knocking on the door with extra ration coupons or to assist in my sewing. I was once again in a community where I could feel and use the positive forces.

By the middle of the season, Jack began to have symptoms of exhaustion. The team was winning, and he was the leading batter and a fan favorite. Things were going well, but he felt sick. Rumors began to circulate that he was on the verge of a nervous breakdown, but I knew better. The symptoms were a manifestation of the prolonged stress he had been under, and so we went for help.

Rachel and Jack on DeGaspé Street.

His shrewd doctor advised a rest away from the ballpark—with no newspapers and no game by radio. Delighted to have him home, I managed to get in one outing, a picnic, before he felt compelled to return to the fray. His loyalty to the team was intense, and he didn't want to be seen as protecting his batting average. The brief respite had been enough to relieve his symptoms, and he knew then that he didn't have a serious illness, as he had feared.

Montreal was idyllic in many ways. Sam Maltin, a correspondent for *The Pittsburgh Courier*, his wife, Belle, and their children became our close friends and companions. With them we enjoyed concerts in the park and small dinners at home, replaying the events of the day. Half a century later, I am still wearing the sweater Belle knitted for me. I can't give it up.

After the Montreal Royals won the deciding game of the Little World Series that year, the place went wild. Jules Tygiel described it beautifully in *The Great Experiment*: "As the spectators poured onto the field Robinson fought his way to the clubhouse to join the Royal celebration. The French-Canadian fans refused to leave, chanting for Robinson to rejoin them and singing '*Il a gagné ses epaulettes.*' When he appeared in his street clothes they gathered around him, kissing and hugging him, and tearing at his street clothes. As they lifted Robinson to their shoulders, tears appeared in his eyes. The crowd remained after he retrieved his belongings from the locker room and they chased

RIGHT: *Jersey City, April 18,*
1946: Accompanying this photograph in
the Jersey Journal, *Joe Cummiskey*
wrote, "Jackie Robinson, first
Negro ballplayer ever to play in
organized baseball, broke in yesterday
with the Montreal Royals—and with a
bang. He smashed out four hits in
five times up—a homer with two men
on base and three singles. He stole
two bases, drove in four runs, and scored
from third twice by forcing Jersey
City's pitchers into balks. Montreal won
14–1. Here's Jackie crossing the plate
after his homer in the third inning."
OPPOSITE: *A portrait of Jack in*
Montreal. I'll never forget the experience
of being embraced by this city.

him deliriously for three blocks as he attempted to leave. A passing motorist finally rescued Robinson and spirited him home. To Sam Maltin, who had shared so much of the magical season with Jackie and Rachel, it provided a fitting climax. 'It was probably the only day in history,' he wrote, 'that a black ran from a white mob with love, instead of lynching on its mind.' "

I was eight months pregnant but determined to see the game. I had to make my way out alone through the joyful chaos.

At the end of the 1946 season, we left Montreal primed for the next steps. The stopover in Canada had prepared us to return to the ongoing struggle for equality in our own country with greater equanimity and a happy time to reflect on.

14

Firstborn

Our son Jackie, Jr., was born on November 18, 1946, in Los Angeles, my own birthplace. Jack and I were ecstatic and in awe of this beautiful child with a full head of hair and big brown eyes framed with thick lashes. Jackie was immediately surrounded by three adoring grandmothers: Zellee, Mallie, and Annetta Jones, my grandmother. He was precious beyond belief and was soon nicknamed "Sugar Lump," a name he bore until his third birthday, despite the protests of my grandmother, who remembered feeling that her own childhood nickname of "Red" had stuck to her much too long.

Being born at the beginning of the blaze of Jack's baseball career and sharing his name proved to be a mixed blessing for this handsome, bright child. He was taken up by Jack's baseball public in a way that Sharon, born in 1950, and David, born in 1952, never were. Jackie was affected more than we knew at the time by being so much in his father's spotlight and shadow.

In the spring of 1947, soon after Jack won his place on the Brooklyn Dodgers, I prepared to join him in New York. I had missed him terribly while he was away at spring training, which I couldn't attend. Jackie was four

ABOVE: *Jackie, Jr., was born on November 18, 1946, in Los Angeles. We couldn't believe the miracle of this beautiful first child.*

OPPOSITE: *Jackie, covered by his beautiful lace shawl from Montreal, is he center of the adoring family, including his grandmother Zellee Isum and great-grandmother Annetta Jones.*

months old when we left my mother's love-filled home in Los Angeles. Curiously, for all of Rickey's careful planning, we still didn't have a home in New York. The acute postwar housing shortage contributed to the difficulty of the search and led to our taking a room temporarily at the giant McAlpin Hotel at Broadway and Thirty-Fourth Street, across the street from Macy's. There we stayed, in the commercial heart of Manhattan, for several long weeks, or so it seemed.

In our room there we cared for Jackie—made formula for him, washed his diapers, played with him—while entertaining reporters who drifted in and out getting their "breakthrough" stories and photographs. My nurse's training helped enormously, for this was a crisis of sorts, requiring rapid, creative organization and self-reliance, too, because we didn't know a soul in New York City. Eating supper involved one of us going to a nearby cafeteria while the other stayed with Jackie. Money was a constant concern.

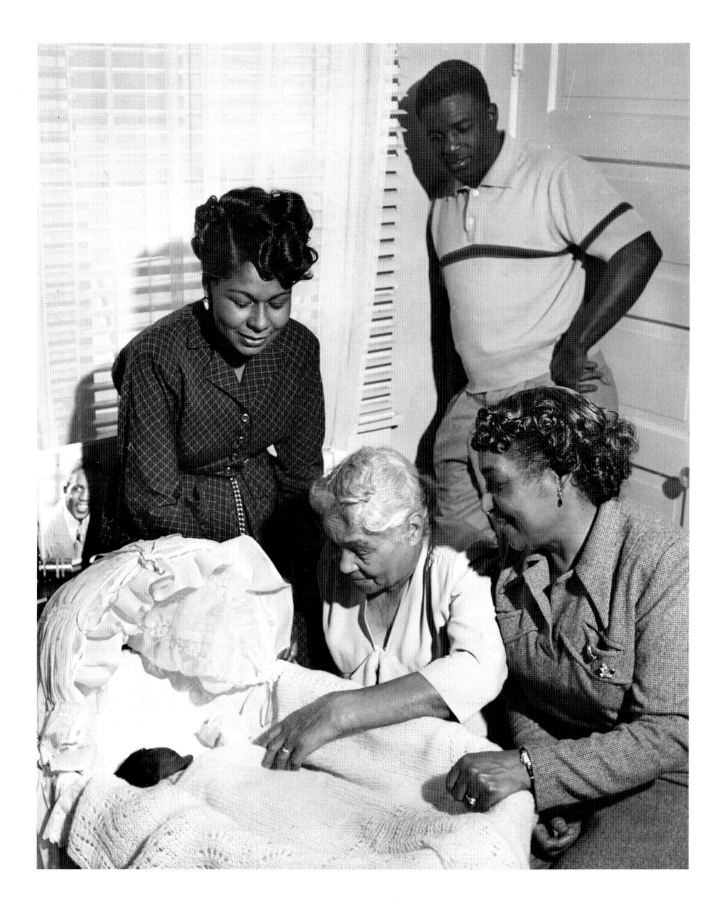

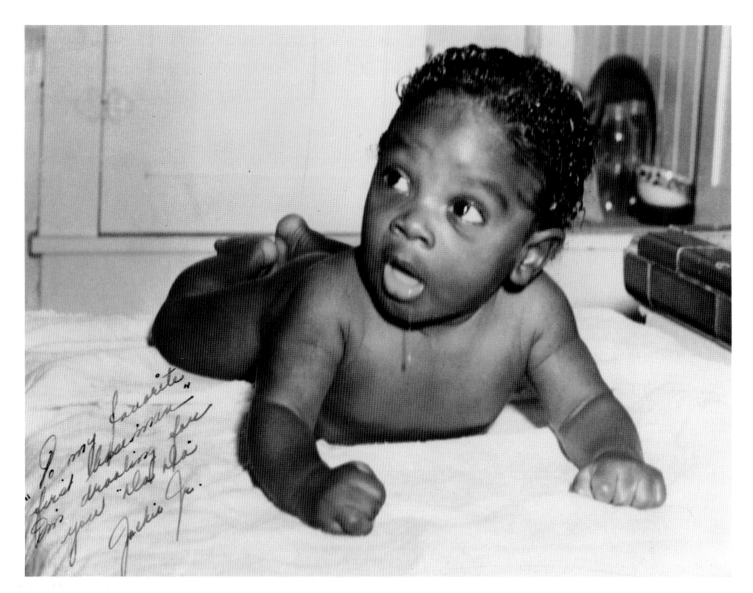

To my favorite "first baseman"—This drooling for your "old man"—Jackie Jr.

ABOVE: *Jackie, three months old and exercising.* OPPOSITE: *Jackie Robinson, Jr., was born five months before his father's greatest trial began. We experienced pure joy at his birth and felt we could protect and guide him.*

Until opening day we seemed suspended in time and space, struggling through the transition and very concerned about the many unknowns facing us.

When the big day came on April 15, I carefully dressed Jackie in the new spring outfit I had brought from California, a lovely light blue suit with a cap to match. I don't recall ever having been so nervous (except perhaps as a student scrub nurse in surgery). Jack had left hours earlier for Ebbets Field. I had to get there on my own. When I reached the street I realized why my anxiety was so high: I had to get to Brooklyn on time, and I had no idea of how to get there. Then I learned that the Manhattan cabbie fiercely resisted crossing the East River to Brooklyn. I felt near panic as cab after cab drove away. I couldn't go on the subway because I was sure I would get lost.

We finally arrived at Ebbets Field, before the game began, cold and underdressed for the brisk New York weather in our California outfits. There, Roy Campanella's mother-in-law tucked Jackie under her fur coat and advised me to heat his bottle at the hot dog stand. We had found our surrogate mother. Looking back, I realize that making so much fuss about getting to the ballpark was my way of managing my greater concern: how my dear husband would be received and how he would perform.

Jackie's First Ballgame

1947

THE BREAKTHROUGH YEAR

OPPOSITE: *In 1947 the Dodgers
held their spring training in Havana,
Cuba, to avoid the racist atmosphere
they'd encountered in Florida the
previous year. Ironically, and much to
their disappointment, the black players—
Jack, Campy, Newcombe, and
Partlow—were housed in separate and
unequal quarters there. Cuban fans
surround him (below).*

ranch Rickey's bold move of October 23, 1945—signing Jack to a contract that would bring him to the Brooklyn Dodgers in 1947 as the first black player in organized baseball in modern times—was a thunderstroke that reverberated far beyond the game of baseball. By revealing that major-league baseball, "our" beloved national pastime, had been deliberately segregated for more than half a century, the signing called into question one of the most cherished myths of American society—that there was equality of opportunity for all of its citizens. This occurred at the very time the country was experiencing a sense of relief at the war's end, and expectations that life would be better for all were high. President Truman's pledge to "help free people maintain their institutions" and to provide billions of dollars to a desperate Europe through the Marshall Plan indicated how quickly the country could stir itself to action. That speed and determination in mobilizing resources was hardly reflected at home in the slow march toward racial equality.

In 1947, as Jack took his place in the batter's box in Ebbets Field, and Rickey watched from the owner's box, the meaning of the moment for me seemed to transcend the winning of a ballgame. The possibility of social change seemed more concrete, and the need for it seemed more imperative. I believe that the single most important impact of Jack's presence was that it enabled white baseball fans to root for a black man, thus encouraging more whites to realize that all our destinies were inextricably linked.

On the personal side, Jack and I began to realize how important we were to black America, and how much we symbolized its hunger for opportunity and its determination to make dreams long deferred possible. We would witness the swelling attendance and thunderous support of black fans as the team traveled around the country. After we moved out of the McAlpin we'd walk the streets of Bedford-Stuyvesant and later, Flatbush, our Brooklyn neighborhoods, and encounter both praise and skepticism. As a group, black people knew we were involved in something momentous, but our racial memory tempered our expectations. In the 1930s, we had witnessed the stunning achievements of Jesse Owens, Joe Louis, Marian Anderson, and many other outstanding black Americans, and their experiences had seemed to promise broad advances. But the social order that denied opportunity to black Americans didn't change. Breaking baseball's color barrier was another chance to chip away at ingrained racist attitudes.

At the end of this season, the Dodgers won the National League pennant and were

Snapshot of J.R., Campy, and Newcombe from the Cuba-Panama trip, 1947.

more powerful and cohesive, and Jack, though beleaguered, won baseball's first Rookie of the Year Award. We felt encouraged by these tangible achievements, always on the lookout for positive signs. Winning meant the possibility of significant changes in American society.

LEFT: *The team at a game in the Canal Zone, March 1947.*

ABOVE: *Don Newcombe, ace Dodger pitcher and good friend, won twenty games in '51 and '55 and twenty-seven in '56. In 1949 he won the Rookie of the Year Award, and he won the first-ever Cy Young Award in 1956. He pitched and triumphed in many crucial games, strengthening the team immeasurably.*

RIGHT: *Jack with Clyde Sukeforth, the Dodger scout who persuaded him to meet with Branch Rickey for the first time.*

16

Breaking
the Color Barrier

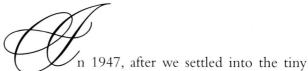

In 1947, after we settled into the tiny quarters we shared with a kind woman on McDonough Street in Brooklyn, life on and off the field became a nonstop challenge to our endurance and will. As Jack crossed the threshold of our apartment and headed for Ebbets Field each day, he seemed to be in good spirits—young, resilient, and striding confidently (in his wonderful pigeon-toed way) through Bedford-Stuyvesant. He appeared to feel supported by the love of our small family and the vocal good wishes of our neighbors.

Through Mr. Rickey's network of acquaintances in Brooklyn's black community, we were introduced to a family who became our friends and extended family in the fullest sense: Reverend Lacy Covington, his wife, Florence, and her sisters, Willette, Mae, Phyllis, and Julia. They introduced us to other community leaders, assisted us by baby-sitting, and welcomed us on Sundays for a delicious meal, good conversation, and the embrace of a loving family. In intimate ways they shared the best and worst days of our lives.

As our private world began to take shape in that first season, we found simple remedies for tension, such as taking long bus rides with Jackie, Jr., to escape from the confines of our too-small apartment,

ABOVE: *Finally with the National League: Jack signs his contract in the presence of Branch Rickey (right) and Burt Shotton (left), the Dodgers' new manager.* OPPOSITE: *After an exhibition game on April 10, 1947, Jack entered the Dodgers' clubhouse as a Royal and left as a Dodger.*

and we grew closer and stronger. Our love and ever-present sense of humor allowed us to keep our perspective and adopt the "wait till next year" outlook that was practically a Brooklyn tradition.

However, every stadium that year was a battleground. For Jack the greatest struggles were internal; the pact he had agreed to with Branch Rickey at his signing—that he would not allow himself to be provoked regardless of the viciousness of the baiting—had to be honored. He could not fight back during the 1947 and 1948 seasons. It was the most challenging and, yes, the most threatening period of his career. All of his instincts cried out for release to retaliate.

From the start of the season, he felt he was a target. Some players—on opposing

teams, and even on the Dodgers—threatened to strike if they had to join Jack on the field. There were deliberate efforts to physically hurt him concealed within the traditional roughhouse tactics of the game: Players slid into the base Jack was covering with their spikes high to draw blood; pitchers threw balls at his head, intending to injure him, not just brush him back from the plate; and the bench jockeying crossed the line from insulting repartee to inciting, abusive language intended to provoke rage.

By midseason threatening letters began to arrive in the mail. Initially, I threw them out, unwilling to take them seriously. But, finally, when one came describing in specific detail the writer's intent to harm us, I started turning them over to the Dodgers, even though I had little faith in their ability to locate anonymous writers.

I couldn't afford to miss a home game; I felt I needed to be there to witness and share in what was happening to Jack. As we traveled back to McDonough Street from the ballpark, we discussed the day's events. We vented our anger and frustration and shared the joy and excitement of winning a game or a new supporter. By the time we got home, Jack could enter in relative peace. From the beginning, he made a conscious effort to join me in creating a haven that we counted on for restoration. In our household, from the beginning of our marriage, there were self-imposed taboos against angry outbursts. I never, ever, heard Jack utter a profane word at home throughout his life. In

Burt Shotton meets his players.
With Jack are (left to right) Harry
Taylor, Ed Stevens, Vic Lombardi, and
Dixie Howell. Jack said of Shotton,
"I liked and respected him. . . . I
appreciated his patience and
understanding as I struggled to get
out of a slump."

ABOVE: *Jack, a Californian, learned to ride the New York City subway.*
RIGHT: *Our beloved friends Reverend Lacy and Florence Covington gave us a sense of family in the East.*

this he had strong views of a man's role in a family. Also, we had both grown up in families in which we had learned to manage anger by isolating ourselves, or by discussing the issue or problem after the first emotional upheaval had subsided. That was our way, with both salutary and costly consequences. However, I learned that there were no such constraints in the baseball clubhouse; Jack was reported to be quite a regular fellow there.

Occasionally I was able to accompany Jack on road trips. When he played in certain cities, most notably Philadelphia and Baltimore, I sat through name calling, jeers, and vicious baiting in a furious silence. My only response was to sit up very straight, as if my back could absorb the nefarious outbursts and prevent them from reaching him. However, nothing could blunt the cacophony of bitterness and hatred spewing forth toward this one man from the Phillies' dugout on their first visit to Ebbets Field. This ugly outpouring was led by the team's manager, Ben Chapman. The Phillies' verbal assault was so excessive and brutal that fans wrote letters of protest to Commissioner Chandler, who issued a warning to team owner Robert Carpenter. Later, in the "City of Brotherly Love," the Benjamin Franklin Hotel wouldn't rent us a room. With as much dignity as we could muster, we went to the local YMCA to prepare for the game.

As the season went on, Jack's teammates—galvanized by his play and the experience of watching a man unable to defend himself stand tall—gradually began to approach him with helpful suggestions.

Pee Wee Reese, a Southerner, went out of his way to convey his support publicly. His gestures dramatically demonstrated what an individual can do. Pee Wee's subsequent recollections indicate the personal growth that came as a result of his experience with Jack.

Perhaps Red Barber described it best in his autobiography, *1947*. Red revealed that he had nearly quit as the Dodgers' announcer when Rickey told him of his plans to bring a black ballplayer to the Dodgers. After a long period of soul-searching, Red decided to stay. He wrote, "All I had to do was treat him as a man, a fellow man, treat him as a ballplayer, broadcast the ballgame." Red did that and more. He got to know Jack; he got to know him well enough to later write: "I know that if I have achieved any understanding and tolerance in my life . . . it all stems from this. . . . I thank Jackie Robinson. He did far more for me than I did for him."

Jack found that the most powerful form of retaliation against prejudice was his excellent play. He "hurt" the opposition by performing well; we knew that achieving one's goals was the most potent method for triumphing over oppressors . . . and he did so with great glee. At the end of this trying yet exhilarating season, Jack received baseball's first Rookie of the Year Award, and the Dodger fans honored him with a Jackie Robinson Day where they presented us with a white Cadillac, a thrill for us—no more riding on buses.

Most importantly, the team—now more powerful and cohesive—won the National League pennant, and Jackie, Jr., took his first steps.

That fall, we went home to Los Angeles exhausted, but relieved and triumphant!

This is a copy of the poison-pen letter received by Warren Giles, president of the Cincinnati Reds, threatening to kill Jack if he played for the Dodgers in the twin bill against the Reds on May 20. Jack's answer to the threats was a big homer in the opener, which broke the game wide open and led to a Brooklyn double victory, 10–3 and 14–4. Hate mail was a crude but threatening manifestation of the potential violence in our situation.

ABOVE: *Jack smashes a single in the eighth inning of a Cubs-Dodgers game, September 10, 1947, at Wrigley Field. The Dodgers won 6–1.*

LEFT: *Larry Doby, a former Newark Eagle star, was the first black ballplayer in the American League. Doby joined the Cleveland Indians on July 5, 1947, eleven weeks after Jack's debut for Brooklyn. Doby hit .301 in 1948 to help lead the Indians to the A.L. pennant. He led the league in homers in 1952 and 1954. A seven-time all-star, Doby also played for the Chicago White Sox, whom he later managed for part of the 1978 season.*

Sliding into second base,
Jack sends Phil Rizzuto flying.
Snuffy Stirnweiss looks on.

RIGHT: *The 1947 season ended gloriously for the team: The Dodgers became the 1947 National League champs.* BELOW: *The honors kept coming at the end of the '47 season. Here Jack Ryan of the Chicago Baseball Writers Association gives Jack an award in recognition of his selection as Rookie of the Year.*

LEFT: *Jack and Jackie at Brooklyn Borough Hall after a parade in honor of the pennant victory. Half a million fans showed up to cheer the Dodgers on.*
BELOW: *Jack greets our mothers, who came to New York to attend the Jackie Robinson Day celebration held at Ebbets Field on September 23, 1947. It was a rousing climax to Jack's inaugural season.*

Jackie Robinson Day: Bill "Bojangles" Robinson, the great entertainer, became a friend during the '47 season. He's shown at right presenting Jack with an inscribed gold wristwatch from Tiffany's, which Jack cherished and always wore. Jack Semel, a season box holder and fervent supporter, presented an interracial goodwill plaque (below). And we also were given a stunning white Cadillac— no more riding on buses. In addition, we received a television set and cash gifts.

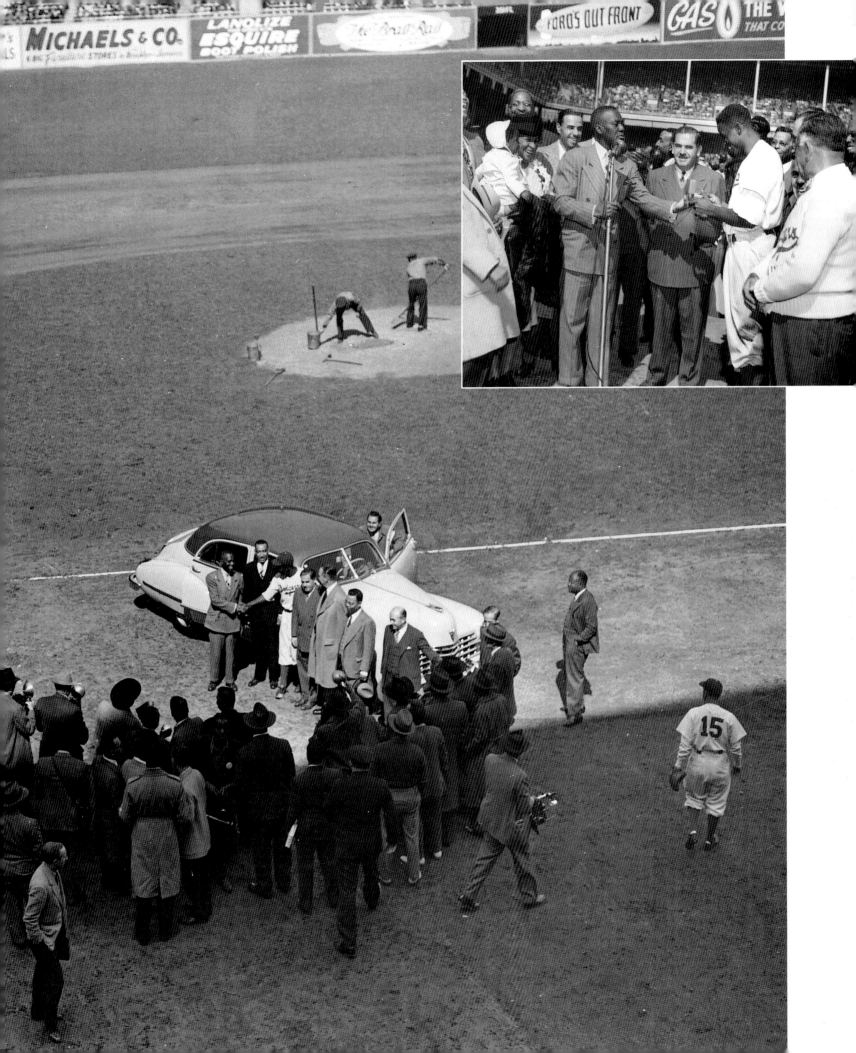

17

1948

N U M B E R   T W O

Roy Campanella and Jack share a quiet moment. Roy's entry into the majors in April 1948 bolstered Jack's belief that integration was here to stay. We were jubilant.

Making it through the first year in the major leagues and completing it with personal honors and a team victory strengthened and encouraged Jack and, I think, Branch Rickey, too. No one believed that racism in all of its destructive manifestations had been driven from the game; far from it. But we did know that there would never be another first year. And we were confident that progress had been made. Once Jack had broken through, and Larry Doby was signed by the Cleveland Indians of the American League in July 1947, other teams discovered that the Negro Leagues had plenty of individuals of major-league caliber and began to sign them to their minor-league franchises. (Ironically, one of the most talented of them all, the great Satchel Paige, was brought to the Cleveland Indians too late in his career to fully enjoy the advantages of the greater exposure—a keen reminder that lost time cannot be recovered.) Still, except for the Dodgers and the Indians, most teams took a long time to go as far as promoting deserving black players to the majors.

Having been in the Negro Leagues, Jack knew firsthand of the pool of talent waiting impatiently for opportunity. And he himself was waiting for the Dodgers' Number Two; he understood that while being the first is important, lasting significance was in producing results beyond his own personal success. So, when Branch Rickey signed the catcher Roy Campanella (better known as "Campy") and the pitcher Don Newcombe, to be followed later by Joe Black and Jim "Junior" Gilliam, all of whom would become cherished friends, Jack rejoiced.

Jack and Campy had first met in December 1945, when they joined a team of Negro League all-stars to play winter ball in Venezuela for one season. At that time Campy was also interviewed by Mr. Rickey, who purported to be recruiting players for a mythical team, the "Brown Bombers," but Mr. Rickey was using the ploy to conceal the fact that he was scouting Negro Leaguers for his real team. Campy had no interest in the "Brown Bombers" and turned Mr. Rickey down.

Unlike Jack, Campy had committed himself to baseball at an early age, and was talented enough to join the Negro League's Baltimore Elite Giants in 1937 at age fifteen. He was an acknowledged star by 1944, when he outhit the great Josh Gibson in a stirring end-of-season duel to capture the league's batting title and its designation as best catcher. After Mr. Rickey signed him in 1946 and brought him up to the Dodgers from the minors in 1948, Roy climbed quickly to the top. From 1951 to 1955 he won three

RIGHT: *Jack steals home against the pennant-winning Boston Braves on September 28, 1948. Carl Furillo is the next batter.* BELOW: *Leo Durocher berates Jack about his weight gain. The manager has the last word on this one— get it off!* BOTTOM: *Burt Shotton seemed to bring quiet stability to the team (left to right): Carl Furillo, Pee Wee Reese, Jack, Campy, Duke Snider, and Gene Hermanski.*

ABOVE: *Rickey, in an expansive mood, holds the attention of Gil Hodges, Gene Hermanski, and Jack.*

ABOVE: *Great-grandma Annetta Jones celebrates Jackie's second birthday.*
TOP: *Jackie embraces Maxine Maltin, Sam's daughter.*

National League MVP Awards and added immeasurably to the Dodgers' reputation as a team that belonged at the pinnacle of baseball.

Jack and Campy had distinctively different temperaments and approaches to dealing with white people. These differences often led to periods of tension between them, usually provoked by sportswriters. Jack was reserved and direct at the same time, impatient for signs of progress, and unwilling to accept affronts to his dignity or challenges to the rights of others. Some sportswriters described his forcefulness as "black rage" and said he had "a chip on his shoulder." Such labels made it easier for these journalists to belittle his point of view. Assertive black men were viewed as "aggressive," prone to violence, and threatening—a widely held stereotype even today. Campy's style and attitude made him more accepted. He was gentler and more accommodating, less apt to challenge. He was described by some as "likable." Although he and Jack were pushed by the press to disavow each other—and occasionally they succumbed—they remained lifelong friends.

The only time I wanted Jack to curtail his anger was when he was challenging an umpire. As a fan, I knew that the game would be less interesting and the chances of my Dodgers winning would be diminished if Jackie Robinson got thrown out of the game. I would try to send telepathic signals to him to calm down, usually to no avail.

ABOVE: *Welcome to Florida! Jackie and I enjoyed spring training in Vero Beach.* LEFT: *From 1946 through '49, we followed the ballplayers' customary pattern of returning home, in our case to California, in the off season. In 1950 we decided to make New York our permanent home.*

18

1949

L I B E R A T I O N

By 1949 Jack had decided that turning the other cheek had lost its nobility, and the effort was chipping away at his spirit. Following the triumphant 1947 season and a so-so 1948 campaign, he had become more and more aware of the price he was paying to be "good," to walk away from detractors, to not retaliate when pitchers deliberately threw at him or sliding base runners tried to spike him. He knew the time had come to be himself, to be free of all unnatural constraints, so that he could play with the spontaneity that freedom brings. There had been no threatening incidents in the stands, and more and more of his teammates and other players in the league had come to accept his right to be there. These were signals that his lack of reaction was no longer warranted nor wise. Jack discussed the issue with Mr. Rickey. I agreed with Mr. Rickey's assessment that to prolong the requirement would have created ill will between the two men. Some have made it seem as if Rickey granted Jack permission to be himself. I would say that Jack had already made that decision on his own, and that Rickey agreed and released him.

On the home front we were making progress as well. In July 1949 we moved into the first place we had of our own, a two-bedroom apartment on the second floor of a house on the corner of Tilden Avenue and 53rd Street in Flatbush. The move meant that we had decided to make New York our home and accepted all the implications of separating from our California families. We felt ready to do so.

ABOVE: *On the stoop of our new home at 53rd Street and Tilden Avenue, Brooklyn, Jackie, Jr., finally agreed to pose after being given a glass of milk.*
OPPOSITE: *Cheering Dad from the stands. Jack won the game against the Giants for the Dodgers with an extra-innings homer.*

Even in this predominantly Jewish neighborhood, we heard rumors of a petition being circulated to prevent our black landlady from purchasing the house we were to live in. By this time we were used to brushing off such cowardly tactics and we settled in, happy to have our lives under our control at last. Shortly after we took up residence, we met the Satlows—Sarah, Archie, and their three children—who had come to welcome us. We exchanged ideas, favors, and child care with them, and developed another lifelong friendship.

Still, with the exception of my brother Chuck's family, the Covingtons, the Campanellas, the Satlows, and the Gordons, we stayed pretty much to ourselves in those

ABOVE: *After being called out on an attempt to steal home, Jack jumps in fury. The Dodgers were in extra innings against the Giants, and tension was high. Gil Hodges looks on.*

OPPOSITE: *Emancipated from the original agreement with Rickey to turn the other cheek, Jack could finally be himself in 1949. Shown taking a long lead off third base, he's taunting the pitcher. He drove the fans into a frenzy by his daring. . . . I held my breath.*

OPPOSITE INSET ABOVE: *In Pittsburgh, August 24, 1948, Jack is thrown out for the first time in his major-league career, by umpire Walter Henline. Coach Clyde Sukeforth was also ejected, along with Bruce Edwards, the catcher (not shown). Jack was fined $25 and Sukeforth, $50.* OPPOSITE INSET BELOW: *Jack goes nose to nose with umpires in another dispute. He could be unrelenting on the field.*

years. Though we shared a few fun evenings with Joan and Gil Hodges, whom we especially liked, there was little socializing with team members except at Dodger parties. In this early stage of our marriage, we developed a style of living that was congenial for both of us. We enjoyed having a small circle of friends and relished spending time alone together in our attractive home with our child, music, and books. The team's monthly road trips were required separations to recover from and store up for.

After our presence in the neighborhood became known, Jack acquired a tiny band of small boys who saw him off in the morning and waited to quiz him upon his return from the ballpark. I was especially pleased to watch him respond to his fans with real attentiveness and patience when they gathered outside the clubhouse door or on our stoop on Tilden Avenue. He could be very abrupt, however, if fans interfered with his meal in a place like Lindy's, where we frequently dined.

The large number of followers was an indication of how popular Jack had become, and of how well the Dodgers were doing in that extraordinary year. They won the National League pennant again and, perennial underdogs that they were, fought hard and impressively against the too-powerful Yankee dynasty, giving rise to the cry "Wait till next year!" Jack had been shifted to second base, and he and Pee Wee Reese became a magnificent double-play combination and solid teammates.

Jack's new, freer style of play brought crowds to their feet or had us watching with bated breath. We were jubilant when he won the National League batting championship (with a .342 average) as well as the Most Valuable Player Award—ironically named for Kenesaw Mountain Landis, who, as commissioner, had kept blacks out of baseball. And most exciting of all, I was pregnant with Sharon. Life seemed very full and promising.

ABOVE: *This is one of the few photos of African-American players relaxing together. J.R. is playing cards with Don Newcombe and Dan Bankhead as Campy looks on. Jack loved cards, a favorite pastime for ballplayers on the road.* BELOW: *Jack won top honors in baseball in 1949. Commissioner Ford Frick presents the much-coveted Most Valuable Player Award.*

RIGHT: *Jackie with Ralph Branca, Dodger pitcher and good friend.*
BELOW RIGHT: *In our trophy room, Jack and Jackie admire the sterling silver bat awarded in 1949 for the National League batting championship. Jack's batting average was .342.*

ABOVE: *Jack helps Jackie light the candles on his birthday cake at our home in St. Albans. Jackie was three, and the happy occasion was shared by neighborhood children and our lifelong friends Sarah Satlow and her children, Stephen, Paula, and Sena. The boy directly in front of me is David Campanella, Roy's son.* LEFT: *July 18, 1949, in front of the Capitol Building. The great artist Paul Robeson, whom we admired, had stated that "it was unthinkable" that American Negroes would go to war against Russia, and Jack appeared before the House Un-American Activities Committee to repudiate this declaration; he labeled Robeson's statement "silly." Jack went on to say that while he was aware of the discrimination, he had too much invested in America to refuse to defend it. Public controversy erupted and, though the majority of both blacks and whites were hostile to Robeson, Jack did experience some harsh criticism. Two decades later, Jack said he never regretted making his testimony, but he did feel he had grown wiser and closer to the painful truths about America's destructiveness to our people, and therefore had gained increased respect for what Paul Robeson had tried to do.*

19

The Glory Years

*Ebbets Field was a special place
for us, like home—welcoming, alive with
activity, a meeting place.*

As we entered the fifties, life felt less hectic and uncertain, and, after the struggles of the late 1940s, our opportunities seemed greater. The optimism we felt was, as always, tempered by the knowledge that not all of the people with whom our destiny was linked would be as fortunate. However, we accepted these years as a brief respite of serenity in order to prepare for a still-challenging future.

During the Dodgers' Golden Decade, from 1947 to 1956, the team finished second in the league three times and third just once, while capturing six pennants. The remarkable run reached its apex in 1955 when our "bums" beat the hated Yankees in seven games to take the World Series, bringing the World Championship banner home to the borough of Brooklyn. Delirious with excitement, we celebrated for days.

In that storied period, Jack particularly enjoyed the managerial leadership of, first, Leo Durocher and Burt Shotton, and then, from 1950 to 1953, Charley Dressen. Jack felt that Durocher was as smart a baseball strategist as he'd ever seen, and he admired Dressen so much that he wore a tie clip Dressen had given him for the rest of his life.

The sense of cohesion and joy on the field and in the clubhouse was reflected in the stands of Ebbets Field. The section where the Dodger wives sat was always bustling, expecting a victory. Our "Dodger Symphony" was loud and deliberately and proudly atonal, always competing with one of the most colorful of Ebbets Field's characters, Hilda Chester and her cowbell, to create a lively atmosphere. Jackie, Jr., was a stadium regular, and Jack would occasionally take him on the field during practice to play catch and take a few swings at the ball. He loved the special attention.

As the Dodgers flourished, so did the Robinson family, blossoming in ways both planned and unpredictable. With all of the incentives of a growing family, we took money carefully saved from each paycheck in 1948 and 1949 and purchased and extensively renovated an English Tudor house in St. Albans, Long Island. For the first time we had a backyard, a play area, sweeping lawns, old oak trees, and space, just as we'd had during our California childhoods. The neighborhood was in the process of changing to predominately black, but at that point, it was still racially mixed. Our new neighbors added to our sense of progress. There were many musicians: Herbert Mills of the Mills Brothers lived across the street with his wife and daughter. The great diva Leontyne Price graced the neighborhood. The legendary Count Basie and his family held forth at the end of the block, and jazz great Illinois Jacquet lived down the street. Other artists

ABOVE: *The Dodger Symphony,*
composed of five fans whose ragtime style
accompanied and underscored activities
on the field. As they drifted through
the stands they added to the spontaneous
fun of being in Ebbets Field.
OPPOSITE: *Charley Dressen was Jack's*
favorite manager. The respect
seemed mutual.

and writers became a source of pride and inspiration as we all worked to improve the neighborhood we called home. Educators Gus and Jeanne Heningburg lived behind us and were my advisers on the educational planning for our children.

The greatest thrill of this peaceful period was the birth of Sharon. I could scarcely believe Dr. Pleshette's announcement that she was a girl. I had longed for a girl as a second child as much as I had prayed for a boy as the firstborn. Like Jackie, she was beautiful, with a head full of curly black hair and long slender fingers ("musician's hands," my mother said of this child who grew up to be a nurse-midwife and uses her fingers to joyously bring new life into the world).

My excitement had to do with the fact that we were on our way to creating a family with the same constellation as my own. A girl in the middle of two boys, I hoped. A girl who would be pivotal at the center of the family as I was, I thought, a girl to be my partner in taking care of the males, and independent in her own right, too.

Well, family dynamics being what they are, and what with the special circumstances surrounding Jack's celebrity and the approach of the turbulent sixties, my fantasy of family perfection was completely disrupted—as Jackie, Sharon, and David could testify. Everyone's struggle was unique.

LEFT: *We had both learned from our families that home ownership was an essential aspect of life, so we felt secure and excited when we bought our first house, on 177th Street in St. Albans, Long Island.*
RIGHT: *Jack and Jackie admire little Sharon.* BELOW: *Sharon was born on January 13, 1950, at Flower Fifth Avenue Hospital. What a thrill to have a beautiful girl! She was delivered by Norman Pleshette, a gentle physician.*

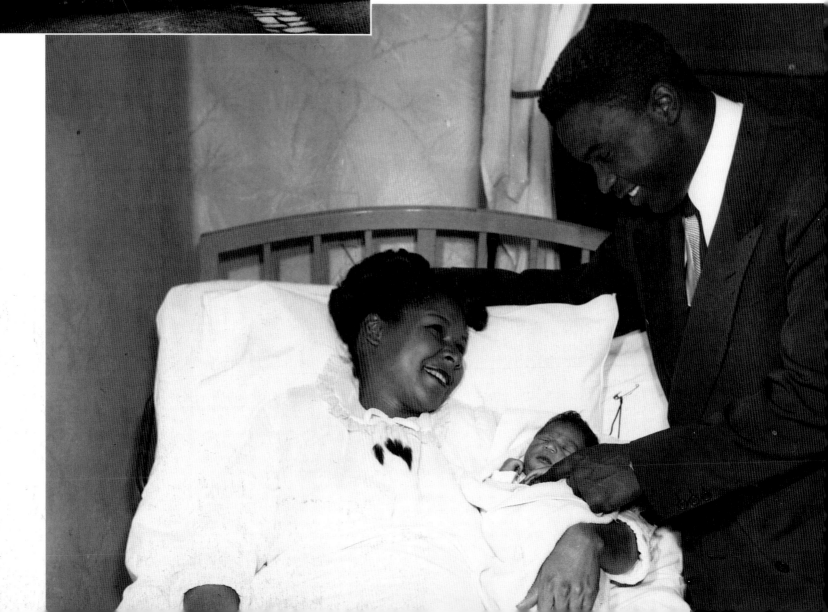

LEFT: *A family portrait in the living room of our St. Albans home.*
BELOW: *That's me at the Steinway baby grand, an anniversary gift from Jack. Although I'm not a musician, music is vital to my enjoyment of life.*

ABOVE: *Jackie and Sharon were
just over four years apart, and as close
as twins.* RIGHT: *Our annual
getaway was to Sheepshead Bay, fishing
for blues with my brother Chuck's
family. Getting seasick was
part of the deal.*

ABOVE: *Jackie, our little prince, with Branch Rickey.* LEFT: *In the early elementary grades, Jackie was quite content in school.* BELOW: *Our family leaving the Covington's brownstone in Bedford-Stuyvesant, Brooklyn. After Sunday dinners there, we were always replete with good food and spirituality. Here we are accompanied by Walter Simms, Jr. (far left) and William Le Grande (top right). William was our baby-sitter for years.*

RIGHT: *A double play in progress.*
Philadelphia outfielder Del Ennis is out
at second, and Jack throws to first.
BELOW: *Jack struggling to score against*
the Boston Braves.

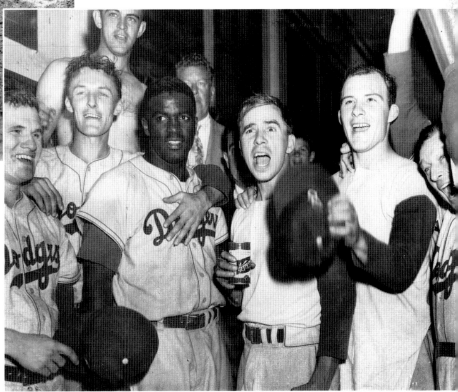

BELOW: *Teammates celebrate a stunning victory after the Dodgers beat the Phillies 9–8 in a fourteen-inning game that sent the Dodgers into the playoffs against the Giants. Newcombe pitched a brilliant relief stint, and Jack made a spectacular catch to prevent the Phillies from scoring when the bases were loaded in the bottom of the twelfth. I will never forget the excitement I felt as Jack hit a home run in the fourteenth inning, helping the team win this crucial game. P.S. The Dodgers lost the pennant to the Giants. That's baseball.*

ABOVE: *The first hit of the 1952 World Series—in the second inning of the first game—was a big one for Jack. It marked his first homer in Series competition. Here he tips his cap and is congratulated by Roy Campanella, next to bat, after he crosses the plate. Yankees catcher Yogi Berra throws a new ball out to the pitcher. Dodger batboy Charley DiGiovanna is running behind Jack.*

RIGHT: *Jack crossing the plate with the winning run. The Dodgers beat the Cubs in this June 1952 game.* BELOW RIGHT: *Heading for home on a passed ball in the ninth inning of a World Series game against the Yankees. Pee Wee Reese (right), who had just scored, and Andy Pafko (waving bat) cheer Jack on. The Dodgers won 5–3.* BELOW: *Irv Noren of the Yankees is an easy out at second in the fifth inning of Game Five of the Series. Jack fires the ball to first in an unsuccessful try for a double play.*

ABOVE: *Playing shortstop for the first time in his major-league career, Jack leaps high in the air to capture a line drive hit by the Pirates' Danny O'Connell. During his career with the Dodgers, Jack played first, second, third, shortstop, and, briefly, even left field.* ABOVE LEFT: *Jack steals home with the bases loaded in the fourth inning of a Dodgers-Cubs game at Ebbets Field on May 18, 1952. Gil Hodges advanced to third, making the play a double steal. Dodgers pitcher "Preacher" Roe is at bat and followed with a rare single, to drive in the final run. The Dodgers won 7–2.* LEFT: *Safe at home! Jack, who had been on second, strides across home plate in the eighth inning after Giants catcher Wes Westrum tried to pick off Duke Snider at third and threw the ball into left field. Brooklyn won, 6–3.*

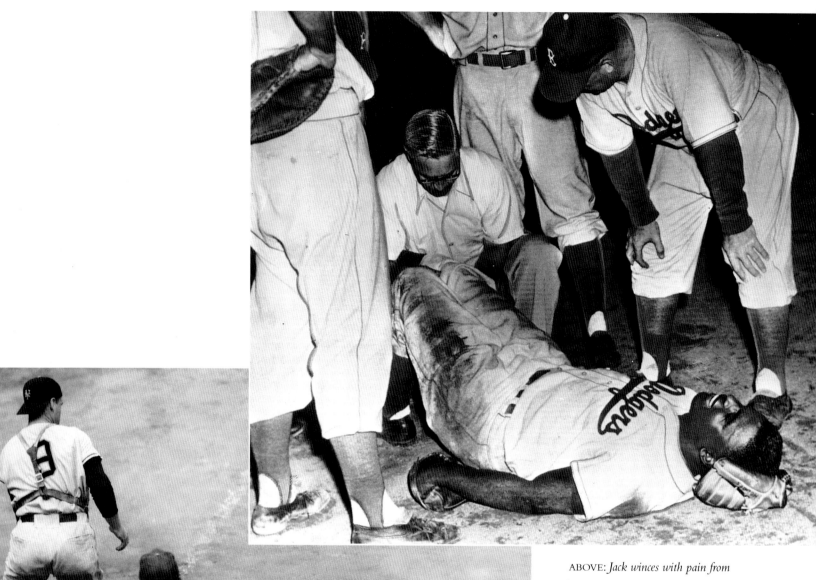

ABOVE: *Jack winces with pain from a knee injury suffered when he attempted a shoestring catch of a low liner. Trainer Harold "Doc" Wendler treats the knee as Manager Charley Dressen looks on.*
LEFT: *Jack kicks up dust as he scores on Campy's double to left field in the first inning of a Dodgers-Giants game at Ebbets Field on August 20, 1953. The Dodgers won their thirteenth consecutive game with a score of 10–0.*

RIGHT: *Jack slides in with Brooklyn's first run against the Cubs on Carl Furillo's second-inning single.*
BELOW: *Jack trots home to an enthusiastic group of teammates. Left to right: Walt Alston, Carl Erskine, Sandy Amoros, Junior Gilliam, Duke Snider, Pee Wee Reese, and Frank Kellert.*

ABOVE: *The 1955 World Champs.*
At last—no more waiting until next
year!! RIGHT: *Dottie Reese*
(Pee Wee's wife) and I compare our
scoring of the game. OPPOSITE: *Jack was*
a sight to see coming off third base
and taunting the pitcher. Here he was
caught in a rundown. Watching this
contest always brought chills,
and I'd pray for a wild throw or
another miracle.

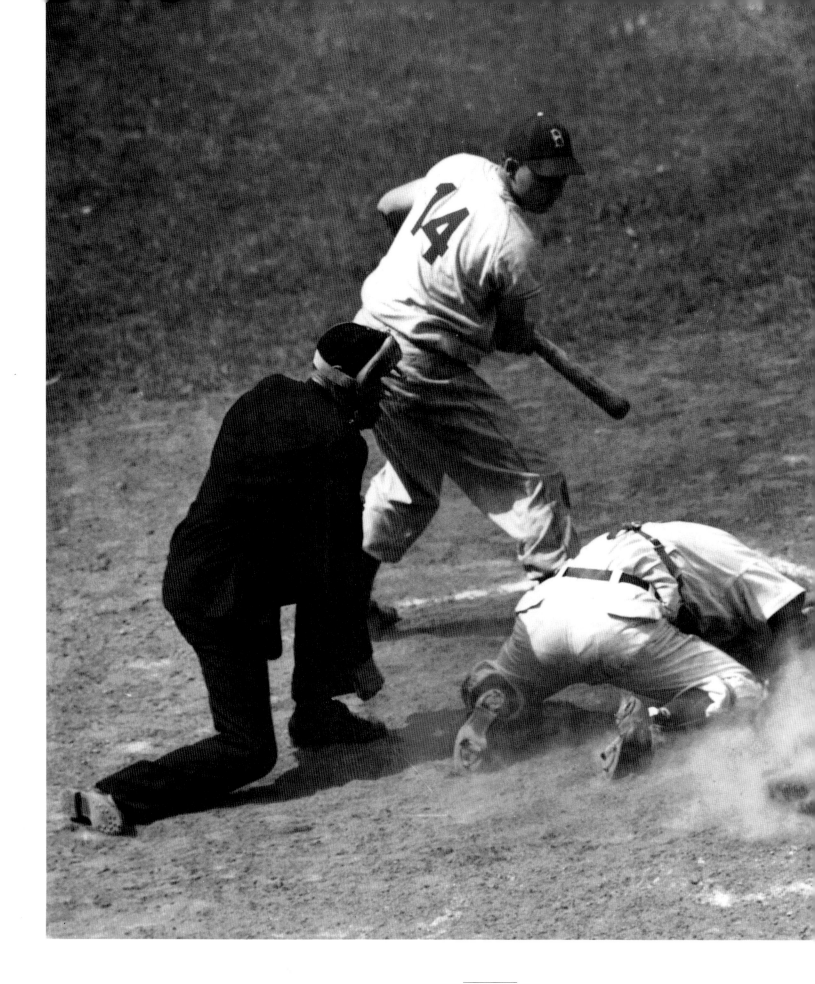

ABOVE: *Watching the World Series with actor Gabby Hayes (far left) and friends. Next to me is Caroline Wallerstein, dear friend and fanatic fan. Beverly Snider (Duke's wife) is on the far right.* LEFT: *In Game One of the 1955 World Series, Jack decided to shake things up to ward off the apprehension of Dodgers fans. The Yankees had beaten the Dodgers in five previous World Series, and the fans feared it would happen again. Jack stole home, beating a hollering Yogi Berra's tag. The daring play aroused team and fans, and the Dodgers went on to win their first World Championship.*

20

The Jackie Robinson Story

*I*n the winter of 1950, just after Sharon was born, Jack signed a contract with Eagle Lion to film the story of his life. He played the lead role himself, our friend Ruby Dee played me, and Louise Beavers played Mallie, Jack's mother. I thought Jack's decision to act in a feature film was daring. He had never acted, learned lines, or been involved in any drama—except the one he created on the baseball field. As soon as Sharon and I were out of the hospital and comfortably settled at home in St. Albans, Jack took Jackie, Jr., and flew to Los Angeles, where they stayed with my family in the house in which I was born, on 36th Place. My mother and grandmother were thrilled to have them.

A part of me hated to see them go, but I decided to provide myself with ample compensation. When Jackie, Jr., was born, Jack and I took turns getting up at night and shuffled through the mornings groggy from lack of sleep. So this time my plan was to hire a nurse to sleep in, and she would have the night shift and I the wonderful days. I'd be rested and able to enjoy a special interlude all alone with my daughter, giving her my undivided attention . . . a delicious thought.

Well, the nurse had been there only a week when Jack began to call more than once a day, to say how much he was enjoying having Jackie to himself, but how much he missed us. By Week Two his messages were escalating in frequency and urgency. Would I consider coming out to Los Angeles with Sharon? He was certain he would learn his lines better if I were on the set. By Week Three, with my pediatrician's blessing, I somewhat reluctantly dismissed the nurse, boarded a plane with Sharon, and flew to Jack's side. So much for the relaxed solo parenting! When I arrived in Los Angeles and saw my two handsome guys waiting, all of my doubts vanished. We needed to be together in this totally new venture, and my mother, grandmother, and other relatives were thrilled to have the unexpected pleasure of seeing Sharon at four weeks old.

Jack and I rehearsed his lines at night, and early almost every morning, a studio limousine picked us up and took us to the set. I marveled at his memory and amazing

ABOVE: *Helping Jack rehearse his script. I was impressed and delighted that he accepted the challenge of playing himself in* The Jackie Robinson Story. *The film was shot in 1950 and is still shown on cable channels four decades later.* OPPOSITE: *Jack rehearses with the producer, Mort Briskin.*

ABOVE: *Ruby Dee played me early in her career and went on to become a star of stage and screen.*
ABOVE RIGHT: *I admire her so.*
RIGHT: *Jack and Louise Beavers, the great actress who played Mallie.*

A *J.R. Story* collage.
Prominent in the Olympics sweater is brother Mack, visiting the set.

self-confidence before the cameras, and I loved watching Ruby Dee and Louise Beavers, the pros, work. *The Jackie Robinson Story* was a scantily researched low-budget film completed between seasons. However, the very fact that Jack played himself made it a classic of sorts. It shows up on late-night television to this very day. Theater audiences cried at the parts where Jack, with great humility, accepted the abuse heaped on him and walked away. His dignity and strength were touching to see. For me, it brought back many painful memories. Jackie, who was only four, and I cried, laughed, clapped, and booed the bigots as Jack performed his acts of heroism and gave brief glimpses of his speed and daring on the baseball field. Jack himself watched quietly, as I remember it, thinking his own thoughts. I'm sure he felt that even a "B" film heightened the awareness of the general public to his struggle.

We had an elegant Broadway opening with friends like Cab and Nuffie Calloway, Hazel Scott, Adam Clayton Powell, and many other celebrities in attendance.

After all the hoopla, Jack just went back to being himself. The record of our adventure was in the can, and we quickly shifted back into our routines. Hollywood soon became a memory.

OPPOSITE: *Standing in front of a marquee on Broadway bearing your name evokes amazement. "How did I get here?" Jack wondered. We were awestruck by this new experience.*

LEFT: *At the premiere, we were proud to entertain outstanding singer Hazel Scott and the powerful Reverend Adam Clayton Powell (above), as well as noted entertainer Cab Calloway and his wife, Nuffie (below).*

21

The Realities

Today, looking back, I realize that no period in our family history was actually as tranquil as I have often described 1950. We had a breather, a quiet time, but there were troubling elements bubbling up. Dissension and protest began to seep into our lives on and off the baseball field.

At the end of the 1950 season Branch Rickey was squeezed out of the Dodger organization and took over the Pittsburgh Pirates. It is said that the death of a part owner of the Dodgers triggered a power struggle between Branch Rickey and Walter O'Malley. In the process, O'Malley acquired two of the three votes and thereby gained control. This occurred as Rickey's contract was expiring, and there were no indications that it would be renewed. After a series of maneuvers by all parties, O'Malley managed to acquire Rickey's stock, and on October 28, 1950, Rickey resigned.

I believe Jack missed Branch Rickey, not in the old role of defender, but as mentor and friend. He and Walter O'Malley, Rickey's successor as president, were never able to develop a comfortable relationship. O'Malley called Jack a "Rickeyman" and a prima donna. Tensions between them surfaced frequently.

In the fifties, Jack began to speak out more forcefully, often representing the player's point of view, as he saw it, and soon was running headlong into the organization. He had confrontations with umpires, challenging calls he saw as wrong (he had a good eye) and in doing so, upstaged his manager. Or there was the time in 1953 when Jack appeared on TV in "Youth Wants to Know" and in response to a question about why there were no blacks on the New York Yankees, said, "I have always felt deep in my heart that the Yankees for years have been giving Negroes the runaround." The comment reverberated throughout the leagues, and so it went: The issue—the real issue—was Jack's outspokenness.

In 1953 the Dodgers refused to extend manager Charley Dressen's contract and hired Walter Alston. He and Jack found it difficult to relate as men: Jack always felt Alston was challenging his integrity and loyalty. I think Jack was rightly proud and protective of his integrity—I have never known a more honest person—but his manhood and integrity were so closely linked that any innuendo struck at his essence, making him

ABOVE: *Gil Hodges greeting Jack at home plate. In his own quiet way, Gil was a mainstay of the team: a slugger, an outstanding fielder, and a man of strong character. Jack counted on him.*

OPPOSITE: *Jack and Pee Wee Reese, teammates in the truest sense, transcended the hate in their environment and discovered the exhilaration of mutual respect.*

RIGHT: *Carl Erskine and his wife, Betty, were a couple we could relate to easily. Carl has stayed in touch in the post-baseball years.* OPPOSITE ABOVE: *Jim "Junior" Gilliam, Jack's roommate, replaced him at second base in 1953. Jack was transferred to third, replacing Billy Cox. Resentment flared up regarding the number of black players in the lineup. Jim, a quiet gentleman, stayed out of the way.* OPPOSITE CENTER: *While Johnny Podres is at bat, Jack steals home.* OPPOSITE BELOW: *Joe Black, ace reliever for the Dodgers, was always one of Jack's staunchest supporters. He often attributes his opportunity to become an executive with Greyhound to the equal opportunity door that Jack opened. Today he is a vital member of the Jackie Robinson Foundation.*

extremely sensitive to challenges. Though I hated to see him embroiled in controversy and misunderstood in the process, I believed in his stance, and later when the civil rights movement began to surface, he was ready; a spirited, practiced proponent of civil liberties.

On May 17, 1954, when the Supreme Court handed down the *Brown v. Board of Education* decision, which outlawed segregation in public schools, and the civil rights movement as we know it surfaced, Jack and I finally felt connected to something larger than the struggles in baseball, more intensely connected to the destiny of our race.

ABOVE: *Jack being hit in the hand by a wild pitch. I always worried about a possible injury and the psychological effects when he was hit—he was a target for so long.* LEFT: *After scoring a run, Jack is congratulated by his teammates. Hodges is behind him, and Campy is in front.* OPPOSITE: *Jack leaps back to first base, just in time.* OPPOSITE RIGHT: *Jack argues with umpire Stan Landes about a decision and is thrown out of the game. The Dodgers still won, 6–4.*

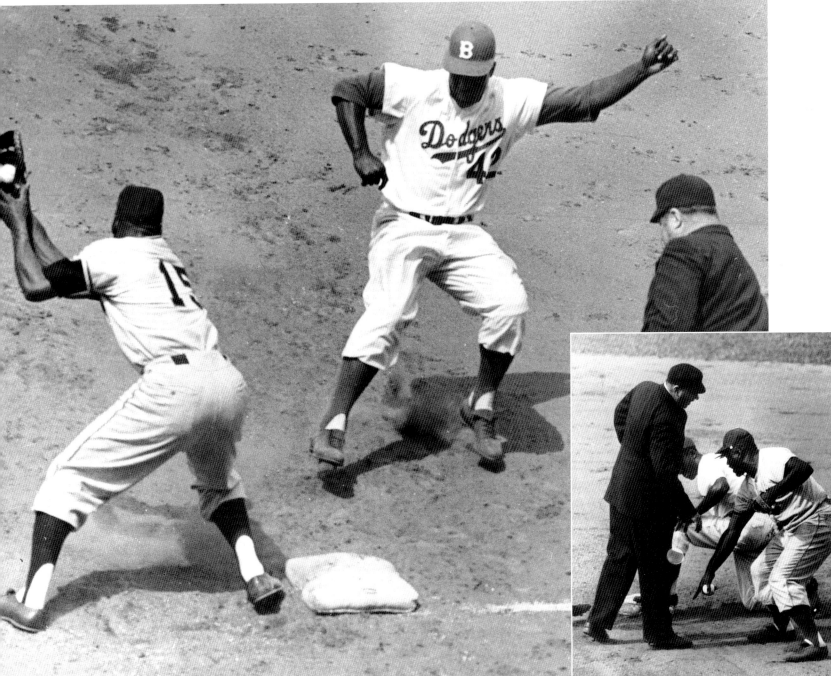

Grossinger's

Star athletes had an open invitation from Jennie Grossinger, the owner of the famous Catskills resort, to visit Grossinger's as often as we liked, free of charge. I doubt that she knew or could have fully appreciated how important the invitation was to Jack and me in the early fifties, as we saved to buy and then furnish a new house. We could afford very few vacations, and there were not many family facilities to rival the Big G, so we were delighted to take full advantage of Jennie's generous offer in the winter months. We started going before Sharon's birth and continued until Jack retired.

We learned to ice skate, skied a little, swam a lot (except Jack, who couldn't tolerate cold water), and ate endlessly. Jack relaxed by playing cards, reading the newspapers in the sunny lounge, or, whenever the weather permitted, playing golf. Although the guests were excited to have an opportunity to mingle with famous athletes at close range—as the management had no doubt hoped—they did so with a courteous restraint that made it possible for all of us to enjoy ourselves and not feel on display. Although winter sports were largely an enigma to Jack, he enjoyed being the proud father and spectator husband. I especially remember the envy he created one year at the ice-skating rink when he repeatedly got down on one knee to help me put on and take off my skates. The women around me would smile and shake their heads. I loved the special attention and, yes, the envy, too. Our secret was that I was pregnant with Sharon and could hardly bend in the middle.

Mealtimes at the G were serious gastronomic events, and overeating was the norm. The generous environment and the abundant display of good food prepared by others made dining a good part of the carefree experience.

It was at Grossinger's that we began a cherished friendship with Bea and André Baruch and their children, Bonnie and Wayne. For a time André broadcasted the Dodger games, and he and Jack became good golfing buddies. After dinner we would all go to the vaudeville shows featuring talent from Broadway, or parents went dancing and children to the movies. By bedtime, with children tucked in bed exhausted and replete with the goodies of the day, Jack and I could celebrate our precious family and our good fortune in the privacy of our cozy room.

ABOVE: *At Grossinger's with our frequent companions and lifelong friends Bea and André Baruch and their children, Bonnie and Wayne.*
OPPOSITE: *Dancing at Grossinger's. I loved to dance with Jack, even though he wouldn't learn any new steps. His fox-trot was well executed, just like everything else he did.*

We long remembered Jennie Grossinger, her family, and such key members of the staff as Lou Goldstein, who brightened mornings with Simon Says, and champion ice-skater Irving Jaffe, who endlessly cautioned novices to bend their knees and always fall forward. The memories of these simple, sweet days helped sustain us when the going got tough.

Jack, the consummate competitor, dares to race Dodger announcer Vince Scully the first time he put on ice skates. I'm rooting for Jack with great amusement.

The first and last time Jack ever tried to ski. Grossinger's was a winter wonderland, but Jack much preferred spring and summer sports.

The family by the pool at Grossinger's. David is in the middle, and my mother, Zellee, and friend Marian Logan are in the background. Notice that Jack is dressed for golf. Swimming, like skiing, was not his thing.

23

The House That Jack Built

*I*n the fall of the 1951 season we invited my brother, Chuck Williams, his wife, Brenda, and their son, Chuckie, to live with us until they could locate a suitable place on Long Island. Brenda was pregnant with twins, and I was carrying our youngest, David. We both had very normal pregnancies and enjoyed comparing notes, managing our combined families, and sharing in the return of the husbands in the evening. Jack and Chuck were mutually devoted, and Chuck became one of the few men in Jack's inner circle.

David was born at Doctors Hospital on May 14, 1952, two and a half months after Brenda's twins. The house then changed from anticipation mode to an infant-dominated dwelling. Willette Bailey was added as nurse for David and lived with us as second mother to all three of our children until the mid-1960s. From his earliest years, David was a bright spirit, even-tempered, fun, creative, and the most adventurous of us all. As the last child born to us, he was destined to be an important source of family strength.

In 1953 we began to feel crowded in our Long Island house, and for the first time Jack mentioned retirement. It wasn't exactly a wish or plan, yet his legs were beginning to hurt, and getting in shape for spring training seemed harder somehow. Also, with the influx of new young families in our neighborhood, the public schools had gone on double session, with duplicate morning and afternoon classes to accommodate the large increase in the number of students enrolled. In fact, there were many ways in which the schools weren't keeping up with changing conditions and the needs of our youngsters. We decided we'd move within the next year or two, and Jack began to discuss the future with his friend and adviser Martin Stone.

I studied the Sunday *New York Times* real estate section with great zest. I loved looking at property and began exploring possibilities for relocation. We wanted to be in a racially integrated neighborhood where we would have space, clean air, good schools, friends for our children, and a strong sense of community. Faced with dilemmas still confronting black middle-class families today, I spent a year searching in vain from Long Island to northern Connecticut for such a place, and in the process I encountered the whole array of discriminatory practices used to exclude blacks on one pretext or other.

ABOVE: *We proudly surveyed our beautiful site, six acres of raw land with great potential.* OPPOSITE: *I worked with the builder, Ben Gunner, in designing the Stamford house. Its openness and glass reflected our California roots. The granite stones came from the property and gave the building a sense of strength and indestructibility.*

A location in Purchase, New York, interested me, but it was taken off the market after I offered the asking price. I knew why, and I resented it deeply. But I had long since learned to choose my battles, so I focused my sights on Connecticut. Now I started thinking of clear ponds, small forests, and beautiful drystone walls; a town with small quaint schools, low pupil-to-teacher ratios, and affordable land; a place with churches and community centers for spiritual development, music everywhere, a cozy library, and, of course, a golf course for Jack. My fantasies of a richer life kept me searching with enthusiasm. It is important to note here that, contrary to the prevailing propaganda that black middle-class families move out of black neighborhoods and attempt to put the

As Californians we were in awe of the magical winter scenes from our balcony.

struggle for equality behind them, we took the struggle with us, consciously and with purpose. With each of our moves, we enlarged our capacities to do more for those who needed help.

When I finally tired of dragging through large derelict buildings in Greenwich, and too-small cottages in Stamford, I began to question the brokers about their preselection process. One readily admitted that she had picked areas where in her judgment my children would feel "comfortable." I wondered how she knew where my children would be comfortable. I suspected she meant not in her backyard.

Coincidentally, about this time, the Bridgeport *Herald* was running a series on discrimination in housing and used our experience as a focal point in an article. Several ministers from Stamford churches reacted to the charges of discrimination. They wanted direct information from me and therefore invited me for tea at the Stamford summer home of Andrea and Richard Simon, a founder of the Simon and Schuster publishing house. After the ministers' departure, Andrea told me she had a plan. Intrigued by her cheerful, conspiratorial demeanor, I learned that she had arranged for a broker to take both of us out to see potential sites—a test for me, an education for her. With the good will flowing between us, we found the site of my dreams on that very afternoon. As we stood together on the sloping hillside overlooking a large pond and a reservoir, all surrounded by trees, we jumped up and down like little kids rejoicing, and it felt like we were old friends. A good omen for things to come.

During construction the family gathers on the boulder destined to be referred to as "our big rock," the site of many confidential discussions over the years.

It was on that spot on Cascade Road in North Stamford that Jack and I built the home we cherished for the remainder of his life. Our contractor, Ben Gunner, wanted the house to be a tribute to his creativity and high standards; we didn't know what we were getting into. On his day off, we would often find him sitting in the unfinished house reading the Sunday *Times*. The fireplace alone took six months to create out of huge boulders from the property. When September 1955 came and school was opening, Ben was still building. Andrea Simon arranged for us to temporarily move into her family's summer house when they went back to Riverdale, so our children could begin school in Connecticut.

Andrea and I had begun a loving friendship to which we both gave the very best of ourselves for a lifetime and from which our families grew in mutual respect. Our children and hers—Joanna, Lucy, Carly, and Peter—learned a great deal from each other, as we shared picnics, ball games, tennis matches, sleepovers, and other events. Together we celebrated family triumphs and cried over tragedies. The friendship Andrea and I shared crossed all boundaries of age, race, and culture, and we quietly congratulated ourselves on our ability to meet the challenges and protect the bond between us as the social changes and disruptions of the following decades tested us.

Meanwhile, as the news spread that we had bought the property, we heard that several families on the block sold their homes. It was described as panic selling. The dentist across the street made a public statement that he would welcome us but that he feared that his property would decline in value. We built the most substantial house on the block, a place of beauty and a magnet for the remaining families, who became neighbors in the best sense of the word.

Celebrating David's first birthday.

Our community activities took place in the Congregational church and community center at the end of the block. Sharon found a good friend, Christy Joyce, across the street, and eventually another black family, the Allens, moved in several blocks away with best friends Candace, Eddie, and Kimberly for our Sharon and David. Our lawyer, Sidney Kweskin, and his wife, Ethel, became our closest neighbors and dear friends, and their son Edward was Jackie's companion until the teen years, when the taboos of society began to complicate interracial relationships. We hosted swimming in summer, ice-skating and hockey games in winter, and football on the front lawn. We served exhausted children hot chocolate in the living room before a roaring fire. I could surround myself and my family with the music I loved—whether classical or jazz—with full auditorium-quality sound. We even got a horse named Diamond and a dog named Rickey to complete the country setting.

The painful side of this move to Connecticut was a by-product of our limited choices. Typical of conscientious parents, from time to time we would agonize about the decisions we had made. While we had acquired a beautiful setting, we had also moved into an almost all-white neighborhood where our small children were forced to be pioneers, pioneers without a context for understanding their plight. For instance, when I went to enroll Jackie in the Martha Hoyt Elementary School, a charming-looking public school in our neighborhood, we had to pass a line of whispering, gesturing, finger-pointing children. Jackie, his sister, and his brother coped with such stresses in their unique ways, but all three paid a price.

My beloved friend Andrea Simon at my home in Stamford. During the thirty-five years of our friendship, we crossed all boundaries to sustain our love and respect for each other. We often walked by the sea, sharing our joys and sorrows.

Though things settled down after a while, there were occasional signs of trouble in our neighborhood. For instance, a friend once attempted to sponsor Jack at the nearby High Ridge Country Club, so he could play golf. He was rejected by a majority vote. An insider informed us that the members who voted against him feared that we would participate in club social events—a miscalculation, as we preferred the social life we had.

On the larger scale—and more upsetting, by far—was the 1955 lynching of Emmett Till near Money, Mississippi. The heroic testimony black witnesses gave, even though their lives were threatened, and the courageous stand taken by Rosa Parks in the Montgomery bus boycott that same year had a great impact on us. We were inspired by the courage and tenacity of these Southerners.

Our identification with the struggle in the South remained strong. With our children settled in Stamford schools, I cried as I watched federal troops called out to protect and escort nine black children into Central High School in Little Rock, Arkansas. In fact, it even occurred to me that our family might have been in a more powerful position in Little Rock than Stamford. In the South, the dimensions of the fight were clear, legislated, and up for challenge. In the North, racism was disguised, denied, and pernicious.

RIGHT AND BELOW: *Stamford was a haven, out of the public's view. We loved our quiet place. We all felt secure in our home and our love for each other.*

BELOW RIGHT: *Willette Bailey and Sharon Robinson. Willette joined our family when David was born in 1952 and continues to be second mother today.*

LEFT: *Weekends were special after Jack's retirement. He liked to prepare breakfast, read, and just sit around the hearth talking.* LEFT CENTER: *This Monopoly group is made up of friends and family who played for long hours. Clockwise, starting with Jack: David, cousin Kirk Williams, Danny Joyce, Eddie Allen, Bradley Gordon, Jr., cousin Rhoda Williams, Jackie, cousin Chuck Williams II, Sharon, and Christy Joyce.* BELOW LEFT: *Jack with our friend and adviser Martin Stone. The occasion was Jack's fiftieth birthday party. On this icy afternoon he did something impulsive that shocked and delighted us. He went outside, climbed into a metal washtub, and went wildly sliding downhill and across the frozen pond. He landed against the bank on the opposite side, laughing and celebrating something personal.* BELOW: *David's class at New Canaan Country School. He composed this verse in fourth grade:*

The Tree
It stands there like a soldier,
Not at all at ease,
While children play around it
In the summer breeze.

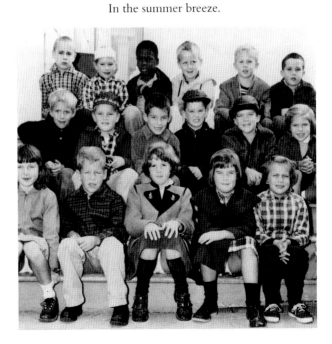

24

Retirement

Jack "stepping out" of the clubhouse and out of baseball after a ten-year career with the Brooklyn Dodgers. He retired with dignity. I felt sad but proud.

"Electrifying" is the word that best describes Jack's entry into baseball. The news captured the attention and emotions of people nationwide. It stirred up old passions and biases and stimulated new debates about life in America in the 1940s. There was celebration in some quarters, new awareness in others, and fierce resistance to changing the status quo in the most recalcitrant sectors. His departure from baseball took place in a mixed atmosphere of triumph and intrigue, a struggle between him and the team's ownership right down to the wire. The issue was whether he should accept being traded, or whether he should retire. It could even be expressed more starkly: Should he quit before he got fired?

At some point in the 1953 season, Jack began to seriously consider retiring. His rapport with the Dodgers organization had deteriorated since Walter O'Malley and Walter Alston had replaced Branch Rickey and Charley Dressen. Also, Alston frequently benched him, which contributed to the feeling that he had reached his peak as an athlete. In addition, he couldn't stand the idea of being traded, of "being moved around like a used car." Age and a very weary spirit underscored his assessment that the time had come.

Jack's fear of being treated like a used car was well founded. In 1956 Mr. O'Malley and company made the decision to trade him to the "enemy" Giants. Typical of baseball and the times, the decision was made behind closed doors; no meetings with the man whose fate they controlled.

Jack best described his final days as a Dodger in his autobiography, *I Never Had It Made*. He wrote, "I met Bill Black of Chock Full O'Nuts. We took to each other and negotiations began for me to become a vice president in the company when I retired from baseball. Also, I was approached by *Look* magazine with a very generous offer if I would give it an exclusive on my retirement story. The time was ripe. However, I couldn't talk to anyone about my plans because negotiations with *Look* and Chock were not concluded. If the story leaked to the press, I would lose out on the *Look* story, and if the Chock negotiations broke down, I would face an insecure future with the Dodgers."

In the end everything happened at once. The day before Jack was to sign with Chock Full O'Nuts and meet with *Look*'s editors, Dodger vice president and general manager Buzzy Bavasi left a telephone message that he wanted to see Jack the next day. Jack sensed the Dodgers were up to something and didn't want to speak with Buzzy

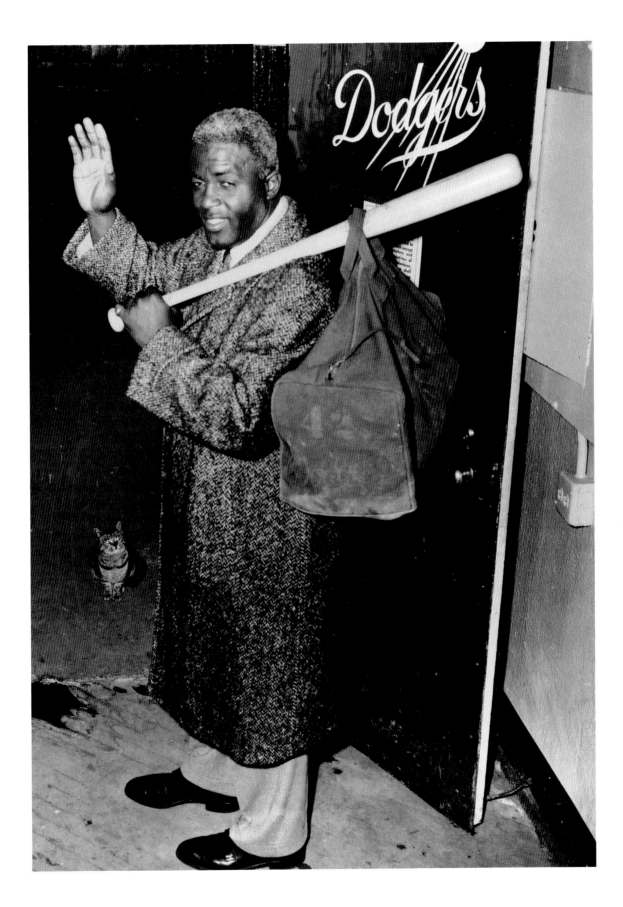

before he was ready to. He called the Dodgers' offices and left word that he'd be tied up the next day. Then, after his contract with Chock was signed, he called Buzzy, but, as he wrote, "Before I could say anything, he broke the news that he'd been wanting to tell me. The Brooklyn Dodgers had traded me for $30,000 and a pitcher, Dick Littlefield, to the Giants. I was surprised and stunned. This kind of trade happens all the time in baseball, and it hurts players to realize they can be shunted off to another club without their prior knowledge or consent. My impulse was to tell Bavasi that Jackie Robinson was no longer the Dodgers' property to be traded. But I had to hold out on that because of my agreement to allow *Look* to break the story. I tried to persuade the Giants' front office not to announce the trade for a few days, but since I couldn't explain why, they went ahead and did it."

The press besieged our home, trying to get Jack to comment, but he said very little. Bavasi and O'Malley sent personal notes to Jack, containing, as Jack described them, "the good old regrets business." He appreciated Buzzy's sentiments, but didn't believe O'Malley was sincere. We decided to go to Los Angeles, to visit our families and get away from the New York press until *Look* hit the stands. But three days before that was supposed to happen, the newspapers had gotten hold of the story, apparently from *Look* subscribers who had received early copies of the issue. Answering *Look*'s frantic pleas, we rushed back to New York to face the press there.

The Giants offered Jack $60,000 in salary, and fans and youngsters pleaded with him not to retire. But, Jack wrote, "When Bavasi told the press that I was doing this to get more money out of [the Giants], I wouldn't give them a chance to tell me I told you so, and my baseball career was over. The way I figured it, I was even with baseball and baseball with me. The game had done much for me, and I had done much for it."

Knowing Jack, I was sure that the public statements didn't begin to convey the complex and strong feelings he had. We talked about the sense of loss, the things he would miss, the things he would cherish, the things he wanted to forget. In the *Look* article he summed all of this up and wrapped it with his pride. He said, "I'm happier than I have ever been. I'll be able to spend more time with my family"—the time-honored vow of men who have been too busy to fully engage in the responsibilities and joys of parenting.

I sympathized with Jack's need to move on and develop further, though as a fan I grieved. I knew that the thrills of watching him perform now would only be memories to savor. I also wondered why the Dodgers had no sense of history and didn't seize the opportunity to make the grand gesture and retire the number 42 instead of trading the man, for thirty pieces of silver.

On September 24, 1957, before an estimated crowd of only six thousand–plus fans, the Dodgers played their last game at Ebbets Field before they moved to Los Angeles, a sad and bitter ending to a vibrant decade.

OPPOSITE: *The joys of retirement! Time for golf, his passion. He kept a putter and supply of balls in the living room and a driving net in the game room downstairs, practicing at every opportunity. He was good—he broke 70!* OPPOSITE LEFT: *Teaming up with sports greats Otto Graham, Don Meredith, and Joe DiMaggio at the American Airlines Astrojet Golf Classic in March 1968.* ABOVE: *Jack also loved tennis. He's shown here with champion Bill Talbert, who was ranked among the nation's top tennis players from 1941 to 1955.*

ABOVE: *The Dodgers were invited to Japan for a six-week tour of exhibition games and sightseeing after the 1956 season. In Osaka, National League President Warren Giles is waving, and Dodgers President Peter O'Malley (in dark glasses) stands to the right. Trip coordinator Sotaro Suzuki is behind Peter. The sign on the building welcomes the Dodgers from the Osaka Yomiuri Newspaper Company.* RIGHT: *A warm welcome to the Dodger team in a Japanese stadium.*

Jack and Betty and Carl Erskine
get a lesson from the geisha dancers. Jack,
who was not known for his willingness
to experiment, was unusually
affable on this trip.

Dodger team and wives following
our Japanese guide, taking in the
spectacle of a Shinto shrine.

Dodger wives participating in a
traditional Japanese tea ceremony. For me
it was the beginning of a lifelong interest
in partaking of local traditions. Years
later I traveled through Africa learning to
appreciate the significance of rituals.
Left to right: Betty Erskine, Carolyn
Craig, Beverly Snider, Kay O'Malley,
and on the right, Janice Roebuck
and Irene Cimoli.

25

The New Challenge

DIABETES

In 1957 Jack, who had always been the epitome of health, strength, and physical indestructibility, suddenly began to lose weight for no apparent reason. The weight loss was immediately noticeable because after his retirement from baseball, he had had to exercise to keep his weight under control. Then, when he also began to experience excessive thirst, we immediately went to his doctor, Charles Solomon, who told us Jack had diabetes. I don't know how Jack felt, for he was completely stoic, betraying no sign of emotion while asking Dr. Solomon specific questions about what he had found and what it meant. I was stunned and sick at heart. I knew immediately that the condition was taking Jack further beyond my protective shield and would significantly restrict what he could and couldn't do. Dr. Solomon fully explained how the disease developed, and he described the proper diet, exercise, and insulin therapy necessary to combat it. He told Jack, "Don't call yourself a diabetic, or think of yourself as one. You are a man with diabetes." I appreciated the distinction, for I have always rejected labels that tend to define and limit individuals. Dr. Solomon had his nurse teach us to administer an injection. Being a nurse myself, I knew the drill, of course, but I sat quietly and watched as she used a tomato and syringe to demonstrate proper technique. I don't remember the rest of that day, but in the weeks that followed, it became clear that the disease and the new regimen would change our lives forever.

Jack set the pace. He told us that he would inject his own insulin, run his own tests, and give up sweets—this from a man who could eat a pint of ice cream at a sitting. It was as close to a declaration of personal independence as I have heard. By radically changing his diet and managing his therapy, he could continue to travel alone if necessary. More importantly, he didn't require or allow us to hover over him or treat him as an impaired person. Although I silently applauded his strength of character, discipline, and determination, I wondered about the grief he felt as he contemplated this assault on his physical integrity. It really didn't matter if his attitude and behavior were based on denial, the need to control, or even just a refusal to give in to the obvious. I knew he was hurt. Maybe the grieving took place when I sat down on the couch, and he silently lay down and put his head in my lap, a favorite position that gave us comfort, but rarely generated words. As he grew older, he kept painful thoughts to himself, and so did I.

The only noticeable change in our household was that we stopped buying sweets and stopped baking, except for special occasions and for the children. I had grown up in a house filled with treats: My mother was a gourmet cook and baking was her specialty. People would slip into Zellee's kitchen at night to be the first to get the last of her cake. Still, the change in routine didn't affect me much, and the children seemed to adapt well. However, I was preoccupied by the little alarm that was set off in my head and soul when I heard the diagnosis of diabetes. It was premature for us to be concerned with mortality—too premature and too frightening.

26

Beyond Baseball

OPPOSITE: *During his baseball days, in 1952, Jack opened a men's apparel store on 125th Street in Harlem. He remained the owner until it was sold in '58. He welcomes teammates Monte Irvin (left) and Joe Black (right), as well as diplomat Ralph Bunche and his son, to the grand opening. Jack admired Ralph Bunche so much he started a fund to erect the monument in his honor that now stands across the street from the United Nations.*
ABOVE: *Haberdasher to actor and friend Gabby Hayes.*

uring the 1950s, Jack became interested in a series of new activities, some off season and some during the season. As the decade drew to a close, I also began to have strong urges for changes in my life. I needed to develop as a separate person with interests, skills, personal challenges, and victories all my own. Throughout the first twelve years of our marriage, I had been creatively absorbed and most contented in the role of wife, mother, and homemaker. I had learned so much from my own mother that I entered marriage skilled and thoroughly committed to establishing a home where love, beauty, comfort, and order surrounded and nourished my family.

My strongest inclination, to create and maintain a haven, was reinforced, of course, by Jack's experiences in the baseball years. He needed what I could provide, and I felt satisfied and important. Being home also allowed me to enjoy my children and support their development. I was one of those suburban mothers so often caricatured as den mother, scout leader, the works: participating in neighborhood drives and causes; racing here and there with a car full of children to events, lessons, games; and present when they came home for talks, snacks, and homework. I did manage to squeeze in courses of various kinds—such as interior design, music appreciation, gardening, and tennis—but mostly I worked at raising my homemaking to a higher level of artistic and spiritual expression. I was the support person so often misidentified as the "little woman behind the great man," but I was neither little nor behind him. I felt powerful by his side as his partner, essential, challenged, and greatly loved.

Jack acknowledged my efforts with constant praise and tender devotion. I had no doubt that home was his favorite place to be. Each evening, unless he was out on speaking engagements, he was at the center of our attention at the dinner table—almost too much, it sometimes seemed to me, for the children and I could hardly keep up with him as we discussed our day. We were close enough that he invited me to ride in his golf cart to be by his side on days off. I was the lone spectator who stopped reading long enough to watch the crucial putt or drive. I was present when he broke 70, a real feat to be ecstatic over. Also, he would convince me to join him at the racetrack by inviting me to "have dinner under the stars," which meant "How would you like to go to Yonkers Raceway?" He was so careful with money and had so few fun outlets, I thought this form of gambling was pure pleasure, and I cheerfully joined him with my five dollars. Once in a

Former teammates Newcombe (left) and Campy and photojournalist and friend Billy Rowe (far right) shared a warm reunion.

while he would walk by the sea with me, but not as often as I would have liked, because being near, on, or in the water is my special passion.

We both focused on the rewards of a more normal life: no more double headers on Sundays and holidays, no more road trips to live through and recover from, having summer vacations with the children and more stability and economic security than baseball provided. I enjoyed these days to the fullest and found ways to keep our family life as undisturbed as possible, but I was caught in the women's dilemma of the times. I was thoroughly seduced by Jack's adoration of me, and my children's growing needs, and I cherished my special position as his wife and their mother, but the expectations that I had of myself had to change, and that was the hardest part.

In 1958, when David, our youngest, entered school full time, I knew that the time had come to prepare myself for the next period of my life. I couldn't be home full time

In 1952 Jack signed a contract with WNBC and WNBT to serve as director of community activities for the station. In this position he was involved in programming, public relations, and merchandising as it affected the local community. The station stated that Jack's office "would provide an important link with the more than one million Negroes in the New York metropolitan area." Again, he set a precedent, being the first of his race to win an executive post with a major radio or television station.

any longer. Jack experienced my move toward greater independence and individualism as a loss—he felt confused and threatened by my ambitions—and furthermore, he felt I was breaking a premarital understanding that I would stay at home. Mallie, his mother, had been overworked, and since his youth he had savored the thought that he would be the sole supporter of his family. I wondered if I had agreed to "never" work? I wasn't sure. Not unexpectedly, I needed greater freedom to develop personally and professionally. I was indeed buoyed by the changing role of women. I knew that what I wanted for myself wasn't aberrant and that women had the right to pursue their dreams. Work and service had contributed to my self-esteem from a very early age.

We talked at length about our future and our differences, and though it pained and upset me to disappoint him, I applied to New York University's Graduate School of Nursing and made plans to seek employment after graduation. I trusted that we would

RIGHT: *Jack also had a radio show for children on WMCA. Here he interviews Cleveland Indian star Bob Feller, who was, ironically, inducted into the Hall of Fame the same year as Jack. In 1947 Feller had predicted that Jack wouldn't be able to hit inside pitching and even declared that if Jack had been white he would not have been considered big-league material.* BELOW: *Jack with his former boss, Branch Rickey.*

work out a compromise. We had created a true partnership, a heady "us against the world" kind of thing, and had been privileged to find a special mission early on. My guess is that we both sensed that finding our way with more separate identities was going to be the most serious challenge of our marriage—and it was.

As our post-baseball lives evolved, I am grateful that we had the ability and courage to openly discuss our conflicts with each other and take on new roles and perspectives without destroying what we had. The baseball years, especially the difficult parts, had prepared us well for the inevitable struggles outside that arena . . . or so I hoped.

LEFT: *Sharing a laugh with actor Sammy Davis, Jr., and welterweight champion Sugar Ray Robinson.* BELOW: *Jack gets some tips from tennis great Althea Gibson. During the two years she won Wimbledon, 1957 and '58, she was ranked number one in the United States and the world.*

ABOVE: *This is a group we enjoyed and respected highly (left to right): Ralph Bunche, Nelson Rockefeller, heavyweight champion Floyd Patterson and his wife, Janet.* RIGHT: *This was a moving moment at a dinner in Washington in November 1953. As Jack entered the dining room, President Dwight D. Eisenhower descended from the dais and met him in the middle of the room. Jack described this gracious gesture as "a great experience" in one of several letters that he and the president exchanged in the wake of this meeting and the violence in Little Rock.*

27

The Larger World

ecked out in his new business suit in 1957, Jack plunged into his new role as Chock Full O'Nuts vice president in charge of personnel with great enthusiasm. He commuted to New York City by car each day, driving the big blue Chrysler with the skill of a jockey riding a thoroughbred horse, using all of his marvelous coordination and reflexes. Jack, goal-driven and determined to master any challenge, took to the roads with a passion. He studied traffic patterns, timed his trips, mapped out several different ways to get to work, and devised ways to set records for himself in the process. (During those early days, he handled money in the same way. He would leave home on Monday with $25 in his pocket, and feel it was a victory to find change there on Friday. He didn't drink, smoke, or have a liking for elaborate lunches, so he found little reason to spend money on himself.)

He applied this disciplined approach to both his personal goals at Chock Full O'Nuts and those set by the company. Fortunately, Bill Black, the pioneering founder-owner, didn't want an officer who was merely a figurehead and supported Jack and his sometimes-unconventional ideas. On January 10, 1957, Black sent him a handwritten note saying, "I'm proud, very proud to have you on my team. I'll do everything humanly possible to make you happy with us," and Jack soon felt relatively comfortable in the corporate environment.

Over the following seven years Black's public and private support allowed Jack to establish his unique brand of personnel management and at the same time engage in activities outside work, even if they occasionally brought public challenges to the organization. For instance, in the early sixties a complicated turf issue arose in Harlem between Frank Schiffman, the Jewish businessman who owned the fabled Apollo Theater on 125th Street, and a black nationalist group. Jack was writing a syndicated column at the time and began investigating the controversy to prepare a report. He determined that, whatever the concerns, he had to speak out against the anti-Semitism

ABOVE: *Coffee at ten cents a cup and tipping not permitted—an attractive offer.* OPPOSITE: *Entering the corporate world as the vice president of personnel for Chock Full O'Nuts proved to be a good move for Jack.*

William Black, president of Chock Full O'Nuts. He and Jack were another fortuitous pairing.

being spouted by the people picketing the theater, and he wrote a piece condemning anti-Semitism. The black nationalist leaders were enraged and threw up a second picket line in front of the Chock Full O'Nuts store on 125th Street. Jack received widespread support from such public figures as A. Phillip Randolph, Roy Wilkins, Manhattan Borough President Percy Sutton, and other black leaders, and Bill Black told the press "Jackie Robinson is right. The pickets can march until they can't walk anymore. They can close down the store, but I am with Robinson." Jack felt that Bill Black's personal history—he was a self-made man who had started his successful business at a peanut stand—had somehow conditioned him to appreciate the struggle.

Most of the employees below the management level at Chock were black, giving Jack an added incentive to represent their interests. He studied wage scales, benefits, training, and mobility patterns, and found there was room for improvement. He visited stores to talk with employees in person, solicit information, and identify problems; the "counter girls," as they were called, were often baseball fans and greeted him warmly. He campaigned for more extensive training, promotions to managerial levels, and better pay for counterpeople, who received on average sixty dollars weekly in the early sixties. And he learned valuable lessons about how working conditions affect attitudes and attitudes affect performance.

Given his accessibility, employees soon learned to bring him both work and personal problems. Since his role had few boundaries, he covered a lot of ground on their behalf: He represented one employee in court, defended another employee trapped by loan sharks, and attended weddings and funerals. Our files are filled with letters of thanks telling poignant stories of his interventions.

After Black nominated him, in 1961 Jack was elected to the board of directors, giving him an insider's view of the corporation, and perhaps more influence, though I was never certain about the power he acquired. In any case, Jack kept thinking of ways to improve the quality of the employees' lives. He decided that they and their families needed a recreational place to go in the summer, free of charge. Thus, "Camp Utopia" in Warwick, New York, was born. Unfortunately, the camp, to which we sent our children for two summers, failed after several years of operation, ostensibly from mismanagement. Jack's idea wasn't well thought out, and my guess is that it was also undersupported by management and they let it fail.

Despite the problems, Jack found Chock Full O'Nuts rewarding. He learned to be an executive; he gained financial reward; he could exercise a certain power and provide leadership among a wide circle of people. He enjoyed the job and clearly had an impact on the organization.

Jack receives a warm welcome as he visits a Chock Full O'Nuts store. He routinely made the rounds to examine conditions in the field.

ABOVE: *Malcolm X and some of his followers join Jack at a counter after the 1960 release of Jack's biography* Wait Till Next Year *by Carl Rowan. I would like to know what was said, because Malcolm and Jack had a running verbal battle, challenging each other's strategies. However, when Malcolm toned down what Jack called the "hate" rhetoric, Jack could appreciate his essential message, and he mourned his death.*

RIGHT: *Distinguished journalist Mal Goode and Jack deep in conversation. Mal was the first black network news correspondent, with ABC. He crusaded for social change, documented all of Jack's efforts, and counseled him carefully.*

LEFT: *In 1957 Jack met with Frank Robinson, who was Rookie of the Year in 1956. Little did they know that Frank was destined to become the first black manager in baseball, fulfilling Jack's last publicly stated wish.*

BELOW: *L.A. County Supervisor Warren Dorn (center) posed on January 5, 1963, with the plan he initiated to build Jackie Robinson Park in the town of, ironically, Littlerock, California. The park was built and recently celebrated its twenty-fifth anniversary.*

JANUARY 5,1963 / ON THE MOTION OF SUPERVISOR WARREN M. DORN

A nine acre site located in Littlerock, California was officially designated as JACKIE ROBINSON PARK.

Jackie Robinson Park
Department of Parks and Recreation
County of Los Angeles

John A. Lambie County Engineer
Mac A. Cosue Chief Architect
Department of County Engineer
Architectural Division

28

The Family Leaves Home

David, Sharon, and Jackie prepare for an outing.

After Jack's retirement from baseball, the family was able to spend a good part of the summer and spring vacations having fun together. Every year we stayed at the Sea Breeze Motel in Montauk, Long Island, with my brother Chuck's family for a week at the beach, swimming, sunning, and catching up on family news. Another favorite outing was deep-sea fishing in Sheepshead Bay, in the New York Harbor area. Jack and I were a bit squeamish about baiting hooks with worms, but the children—especially the boys—loved it.

The school year, however, brought its share of challenges. In sixth grade, school officials had placed Jackie in a track for slow readers, a discouraging move loaded with negative signals. I visited his school frequently, attempting to support him as much as possible, but I didn't challenge the decision. Even as a parent-advocate, I felt helpless to effectively challenge the tracking system. That wasn't done in those days, especially in such a seemingly benign school. The best I could do was to arrange for tutoring and stay close to him so that he would know that Jack and I had confidence in him.

He was brave enough to play baseball in the Little League in elementary school and in the Babe Ruth League through junior high school. But he was haunted by insensitive adults in the stands who would holler, "Your dad could have beat that out" or "Jackie Robinson would have made that play." Jackie persisted nonetheless. He was forced to endure in other ways, too, because he was the only black child in his school and in the immediate neighborhood during his preadolescent years. Most of his childhood peers were congenial, and he was always welcome at the homes of two of his classmates who lived in our area. But the pressure that he felt at always being compared to his famous father, and the importance that the lack of "appropriate" girls to date assumed as adolescence approached, left him socially isolated and feeling very alone.

Sharon, a conscientious student, joined the Girl Scouts, tried ballet, and played the flute with her friend Christy, her white schoolmate who lived across the street. But in 1962, as their junior high school years ended and high school loomed, they drifted apart. Jack and I wondered if the break, which seemed to be entirely Sharon's choice, stemmed from the intense attention she was paying to the country's turmoil over civil rights or if

Mallie Robinson with two powerful men, light heavyweight champ Archie Moore and heavyweight champ Jersey Joe Walcott. When Mallie stopped working and began to step out, she dressed to fit this new stage of her life.

she thought that she and Christy would be separated as dating began. We suspected it was the latter, but she tended to keep her concerns to herself. Sharon and Candace Allen, the daughter of the only other black family in our area of Stamford, became best friends and embarked on their social life in black and white settings together.

Having seen the tensions Jackie and Sharon encountered in the Stamford public schools, we decided to enroll David in a private school, New Canaan Country School, in the first grade. It was all white, too, but we felt that it offered superior educational opportunities, smaller classes, and a richer array of extracurricular activities.

David had to create his own place there by selecting friends and by joining in such activities as soccer and ice hockey. He also developed his own sense of himself through writing poetry that was often intensely personal. In one poem entitled "The Tree," he described the oak tree (himself) as standing tall while the children circled around it. He conveyed the thought that he managed his isolation by fiercely holding on to a positive identity and feeling of relative strength—a precocious notion for a seven year old. His intimate relationships with Eddie Allen, Mike Colhoun, and others, and his devotion to riding and caring for our horse, Diamond, provided rich spiritual nourishment.

Thinking back, I can't recall that we ever used our gathering around the dinner table each evening to explicitly discuss the social landscape or analyze the undercurrents and the practices that the children might encounter. We talked about how to address the teacher, find the bathroom, and behave, but gave them few instructions on how to defend themselves. Jack and I got them the books, bags, clothes, haircuts, and other things they needed as the material evidence of belonging. We supported their natural optimism, their belief in fairness, honor, the code of merit, and the need to earn respect, and we hoped the lessons they heard in our Congregational church reinforced our spiritual and ethical teachings. Our faith was that just as we had learned to make our way in the world by watching our parents and grandparents and the community at large and by relying on ourselves, so our children would find observation and practice, not didactic discussion, the best teacher. We learned belatedly that our children needed to be encouraged to speak more explicitly with us about the realities of their situation as they saw it. They handled their dilemmas in silence.

It was in this climate that I was admitted to the graduate program in psychiatric nursing in 1959, and I was anxious on a number of levels. The children were reluctant to let me go out of fear of "losing" me, and I wondered if I was "abandoning" them. I was thirty-seven years old, and feeling older as I contemplated competing with students who didn't have my responsibilities to pull them away from their studies. I had some doubts about my ability to compete. I felt that my head was filled with child-care concerns and instructions for my mother, who had come to live with us. I wondered if I would be able to concentrate on learning theories and concepts. However, I was extremely excited by the prospect.

My first day at NYU seemed to put an exclamation point on my anxiety. I had gone to the university co-op and purchased all the required books, as well as several reference works for my home library. The armful of volumes comforted me—I could pretend that they contained all of the answers. I stood in front of the elevator on my way to my first class. As the door opened and discharged a load of laughing, bright-eyed "kids," I suddenly dropped my entire stack of books, thereby reducing myself to the stature I feared—a helpless and befuddled "old lady." Students stopped and helped with sympathetic smiles, but I thought I detected ridicule in their eyes as well. But once classes started, all discomfort disappeared and soon I began to realize that as well as giving me the maturity to face this period in my life, my twelve years of homemaking were the perfect preparation for all of the elements of the coursework that I had come to study. I had been functioning in a small group (the family), I had been studying growth and development (the children), I had first-hand experience with human behavior and personality development, and so on. In fact, I had life experience in everything except statistics, which was rough. However, I got good grades throughout and expanded my horizons and skills.

To my delight and surprise, Jack joined me in a way that was vital to my enjoyment of the student's life. When I had night classes, he would wait for me at the Chock Full O'Nuts store nearest the Washington Square campus. As we drove home together and shared our experiences of the day, I felt we were close in a new way. It seemed that he had accepted that it was his turn to support me, at least through the student phase. Having him waiting for me was reminiscent of our youth and courting at UCLA. Ever the romantic, I loved just the sight of him waiting patiently for me to arrive.

Managing the combination of family life and study wasn't easy, but it did make me

Jack believed that positive relations between blacks and Jews were critical to both.

feel fortunate and proud of myself. Still, there was a lingering problem I needed to work on. Through all of the clinical settings where I was being trained, I managed to keep my Jackie Robinson connection a secret. Like my children, I wanted to make my own way and be appreciated on my own merits. In my last setting, at Creedmore State Hospital, I was studying group therapy and was the group leader on the men's ward. One day a patient said, "Nurse, you look just like a picture I saw in *Look* magazine of Jackie Robinson's wife. Are you?" Startled by the question—and despite the warning of my supervisor, Dr. Peter Lacquer, never to lie to patients—I said "No," and continued on, painfully aware of the man's confusion and incredulous stare. I was embarrassed and annoyed, but the encounter helped me realize that I would have to learn how to be both my selves without letting "Mrs. Jackie Robinson" overshadow "Rachel Robinson."

Beloved family—my brother Chuck
Williams and his wife, Brenda.

Jack's best friends "Little Jack"
and Bernice Gordon, with their
granddaughter, Jill.

29

Speaking Out

THE NAACP

By 1957 the momentum of the civil rights movement had increased sharply. The Southern Christian Leadership Conference (SCLC), with Martin Luther King, Jr., as its head, had been organized to directly challenge segregation throughout the South. Congress had passed civil rights legislation for the first time since the Reconstruction, and the school desegregation crisis in Little Rock, Arkansas, where Thurgood Marshall and the NAACP Legal Defense Fund were helping Daisy Bates and the local black community desegregate the public schools, was exploding. In the summer of 1960, student-led sit-ins occurred all through the South, sponsored by the Student Non-Violent Coordinating Committee and the NAACP.

Jack, as excited as all of us by these signs of progress, wanted to participate in a meaningful way. He was drawn to the NAACP, whose history as an effective force was unmatched.

So, he accepted immediately when Roy Wilkins, executive director of the NAACP, asked him to serve as chairman of the organization's million-dollar Freedom Fund Drive. He knew the challenge would be in speaking before diverse groups across the country and representing an organization whose work he respected but whose history was only vaguely familiar to him. Bill Black supported Jack's involvement. On behalf of the employees of Chock Full O' Nuts, he presented Jack with a check for $10,000 for the campaign. Roy Wilkins recruited Franklin Williams, a brilliant lawyer who had worked with Thurgood Marshall and other NAACP luminaries, to accompany Jack. Their pairing on the cross-country journey proved as memorable to both of these assertive men as their eventual success in meeting the goal. Jack was a celebrity with charm, fervor, and a strong commitment to the cause. Frank was a brilliant and seasoned lawyer, a veteran in the civil rights movement, skilled in the art of fund-raising. To Frank's surprise, Jack quickly learned to speak well and knowledgeably about their mission, and they developed into a smoothly functioning team. On the road, Jack, a quick study, began to incorporate portions of Frank's speeches in his own appeal, making it necessary for Frank to create new material as they progressed, an unexpected challenge to which he rose with good humor.

The synergy between the men was exhilarating and effective. They reached the

ABOVE: *Lawyer, civil-rights activist, and dear friend Franklin Williams receiving the Jackie Robinson Foundation's Founders Award in 1988.* OPPOSITE: *Jack, an active member of the NAACP national board of directors, displays the association's '62 subway membership poster. It helped secure the 500,000 new members needed that year.*

Three great men—Robinson, Marshall, and Wilkins—passionately committed to social equality and effective agents of change. Marshall became the first African-American Supreme Court justice on October 2, 1967.

point in their meetings when people in churches would come down aisles waving bills and joining in the spirit they created. This powerful experience of collaborating for the good of the movement formed the basis of a lifelong relationship of mutual admiration and respect. In later years, Frank went on to become the special assistant to Sargent Shriver, director of the Peace Corps, United States ambassador to Ghana, and finally president of the Phelps Stokes Fund.

Jack followed this early experience with numerous other campaigns and fund-raising drives for the NAACP. He served on the board of directors until 1967, when he regretfully resigned because he felt "disenchanted" that the leadership "had become a reactionary and undemocratic political group," stifling the efforts of younger, more progressive members. It was a decision he later regretted, feeling that he should have stayed on to fight from within.

30

Man of Honors

After he retired from baseball, Jack was showered with honors. The recognition took many forms, including honorary degrees from the University of Maryland, Franklin Pierce College, Sacred Heart University, Pace University, and Howard University; a citation from the National Conference of Christians and Jews; and the Two Friends Award of the National Urban League, given to him and Branch Rickey. The honors continued to come posthumously. In 1984 President Reagan awarded Jack the Medal of Freedom, the nation's highest civilian award. The citations, plaques, and trophies filled a large room in our Stamford house.

Jack was always delighted by these tributes: To him they indicated society's acknowledgment of not just his own good deeds, but of the achievements of African-American people as a group. That was why the NAACP's prestigious Spingarn Medal, which the organization awarded for distinguished service to black America, was the civic honor he prized most. Given to him in December 1956, the year he retired from baseball, it confirmed Jack's beliefs that his accomplishments on the field had significance beyond sports—and that he himself was needed in the ranks of black leadership.

I attribute the wonder he experienced as group after group saluted him to one of his least publicly recognized traits—his humility. I admired this characteristic when I first met him, and I watched it develop and deepen as he matured. I am convinced that this humility stemmed from both his religious faith and his sense of himself, for he often told me that he believed he had been endowed with talent to be of service to others. This was not vanity; Jack was not one to brag. It was a principle Mallie had instilled in him early in life. Those of us who were close to Jack grew to appreciate his lack of arrogance (to me, associated with insecurity), and we celebrated the strong, humble man. This humility I speak of was neither meek nor modest, and certainly not lacking in pride; rather it was a virtue based on strong self-esteem and a powerful sense of personal and group destiny.

Of course, the prize he most coveted and agonized over was election to the Baseball Hall of Fame, the game's highest honor: Jack wanted to be elected not because he was the black man who had cracked baseball's color line, but because he excelled at the standards applied to all. To be elected, a player had to be out of the game for five years and then get seventy-five percent of the votes of the members of the Baseball Writers' Association. That was the source of Jack's worry, which grew noticeably in 1962, his first

RIGHT: *Just prior to Jack's induction into the Hall of Fame, Martin Luther King sponsored a dinner in his honor. Among those in attendance were these men, who had inspired and supported him: Governor Nelson Rockefeller, Ralph Bunche, William Black, and Branch Rickey.* BELOW: *Our friend and civil-rights activist Arthur Logan, M.D., the distinguished educator Dr. Benjamin Mays, and jazz great Lionel Hampton (with Governor Nelson Rockefeller) also attended.*

ABOVE: *Together again.*
BELOW: *Jack's mother, Mallie, and sister,*
Willa Mae (flanking my mother,
Zellee), savor the day.

ABOVE: *Jack was thrilled to have*
Branch Rickey and his mother share the
day with us. He paid tribute to each
of us, and we basked in the reflected
glory of his achievements.

The citation reads:

Jack Roosevelt Robinson

Brooklyn N.L. 1947 to 1956

Leading N.L. batter in 1949. Holds

fielding mark for second baseman

playing in 150 or more games with

.992. Led N.L. in stolen bases in

1947 and 1949. Most Valuable

Player in 1949. Lifetime batting

average .311. Joint record holder for

most double plays by second

basemen, 137 in 1951. Led second

basemen in double plays

1949–50–51–52.

year of eligibility. As the time for the balloting approached, he wondered if the strained relations he had had with some sportswriters would now work against him. In his autobiography he wrote, "I steeled myself for rejection." But he was not rejected. The vote was a "squeaker"—he received 124 votes out of a possible 160, or 77.5 percent.

We were at home in Stamford on January 23, 1962, when word of his election reached us. We were jubilant and joyful as we entertained the press streaming through our home. Being a determined optimist, I had anticipated his election, but I still felt relieved. There were few things Jack would openly admit he wanted, and this was one of them.

Jack's personal triumph was made all the sweeter when the Southern Christian Leadership Conference sponsored an elegant testimonial dinner in his honor at the Waldorf-Astoria Hotel in New York in July. There the throng, which filled the ballroom to capacity (Jack had asked that all the proceeds go to SCLC's voter registration drive in the South), gathered to hear Martin Luther King declare that Jack's achievements had

In 1971 Jack and I were honored to receive the PUSH (People United to Serve Humanity) Humanitarian Award from Reverend Jesse Jackson and Reverend Willie Barrow. Jack served on the PUSH board of directors and early on identified Reverend Jackson as a leader with great potential.

On June 7, 1957, Jack received the honorary degree of Doctor of Laws from Howard University. The citation reads in part: "Jackie Robinson, Howard University has invited you here today in order to express to you her esteem and affection for you as a sportsman and a man. It was your remarkable ability as a sportsman and your remarkable self-control as a man which made possible the effective beginning of a major revolution in American baseball—a revolution which has popularized and strengthened beyond measure our deepest American faith: our faith in the open door of equal opportunity for every human being, whatever his race or color, religion or national origin." Dr. Martin Luther King, who also received a degree that day, joined the procession.

created "a rich legacy of confidence and hope" for yet-unborn generations of African-Americans. Unfortunately, King's speech was read for him after he was called home for an emergency. Nonetheless, the dinner was a stunning prelude to the induction ceremonies in quaint Cooperstown, New York, on July 23.

The day was overcast and gray. But that didn't dampen the enthusiasm that ran like a current through the crowd of five thousand who had gathered to see Jack and Bob Feller inducted. Jack, in a voice filled with emotion, told the attentive audience, "Today everything is complete. I could not be here without the advice and guidance of three of the most wonderful people I know. My adviser and wonderful friend . . . a man who has treated me as a father . . . Branch Rickey. My mother, Mrs. Mallie Robinson, and my wife, Rachel Robinson. I've been riding on clouds since the election and I don't think I'll come down." Cartons of letters, telegrams, and special tributes arrived at our home from friends, fans, and officials alike. Jack could breathe easier and feel proud. He had stayed true to his principles and mission, and he had triumphed.

31

The Turbulent Sixties

The induction into the Hall of Fame occurred during a period of great changes and challenges in our own lives as well as the nation's. We all felt closely connected to the civil rights activists in the South; they were carrying forward the historic struggle for freedom that Jack himself had been one of the heroes of for almost two decades. Ahead—who could have guessed!—were years of far greater turbulence, in which the war in Vietnam, and the assassinations of John F. Kennedy, Malcolm X, Martin Luther King, and Robert F. Kennedy, would test the fabric of the nation, and test the strengths of our own souls, too. Even in 1962, it was clear that each of us in the Robinson family was becoming more independent, and that this was changing how we dealt with each other.

After getting my master's degree from New York University in 1960, I became a psychiatric nurse in a research program conducted by the Albert Einstein College of Medicine Department of Social and Community Psychiatry. As a member of an interdisciplinary team headed by Dr. Israel Zwerling, I helped create and operate the first day hospital in America for acutely ill psychiatric patients. My colleagues Audrey Ballard, R.N., Mel Roman, Ph.D., Saul Schiedlinger, Ph.D., Harris Peck, M.D., Jack Wilder, M.D., and others, shared the challenge and exhilaration of being on the cutting edge of a pioneering effort begun in England.

During my five years at Einstein, I found my work with patients deeply engrossing and satisfying. Our goal was to determine which patients, under what circumstances, could live at home and be effectively treated in a community setting. We demonstrated that approximately eighty percent of the patients who had families willing to join in the treatment program could be maintained in a day hospital. In 1965 this form of treatment showed great promise, but it required funding sources to commit fully to the concept and establish community facilities. That didn't happen. Today, as we witness the consequences of this kind of failed public policy, we see the crisis of seriously ill people wandering through the streets homeless and neglected.

My new schedule involved me in the exodus of the Robinson family every morning. We were all going our own ways. Jack and I were developing separate interests and associates in the workplace, which added a new dimension to our marriage. The task for us as a family was to maintain our closeness as we grew as individuals.

My mother took on added responsibilities with zest. She happily shopped and pre-

ABOVE: *The integration of Central High School in Little Rock was a big story abroad on September 25, as this montage of headlines from London papers shows. Radio Moscow said: "It is hard to realize that all this is taking place in a country proclaiming its democratic liberties for all to hear."*
OPPOSITE: *In April 1960 Jack joined the picketing in front of a Cleveland branch of W.T. Grant, a store that refused to serve Negroes at the lunch counter in the South. The action was organized by the NAACP.*

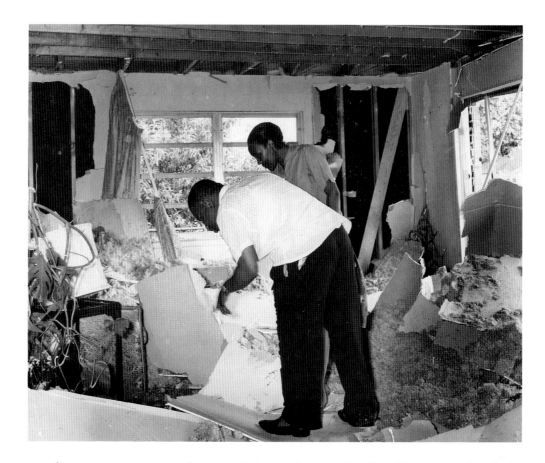

The home of Reverend Fred Shuttlesworth, the spiritual leader of Birmingham's black community, was bombed and completely destroyed on December 25, 1956, arousing great anger and a desire for confrontation in that city.

pared gourmet evening meals on weekdays and escaped to Brooklyn on weekends for her social life. Although Jack and I were commuting separately, we both made getting home early a priority. Somehow the evening gathering with a loving grandmother to feed us and listen to our tales gave us a feeling of solidarity. It was one of those rich and harmonious periods in life, topped off by our participation, as a family, in the March on Washington for Jobs and Freedom on August 28, 1963. Standing before the Lincoln Memorial shoulder to shoulder with hundreds of thousands of people protesting with strength and dignity was a glorious experience. Martin Luther King's "I Have a Dream" speech was the highlight of the day. On that day we reached the heights of emotion and left filled with hope and pride.

Meanwhile, the pivotal presidential contest between Richard Nixon and John F. Kennedy in 1960 had fully engaged Jack's interest in politics. A registered Independent, Jack had supported Hubert Humphrey's campaign for the Democratic nomination—he wholeheartedly admired his position on civil rights and other issues when he was mayor of Minneapolis and a U.S. Senator. When Humphrey lost to Kennedy, Jack studied Kennedy's and Nixon's records and also met privately with the two men. In explaining his choice of Nixon, he wrote, "As Vice President and as Presiding Officer of the Senate he had a fairly good track record on civil rights." On the other hand, Jack left his meeting with John Kennedy distrusting the candidate. He felt that Kennedy seemed uncomfortable during their discussion and was dismayed by Kennedy's admitted lack of

Jack and Reverend Wyatt T. Walker inspect the charred wreckage of the Mount Olive Baptist Church in Sasser, Georgia. This church, along with another at the Chickasawhatche community, was burned to the ground early September 9, 1962, in what was apparently another racial incident in this already tense area.

understanding of the problems of black people. Jack wrote, "Although I appreciated his truthfulness, I was appalled that he could be so ignorant of our situation."

Jack began to lose confidence in Nixon when he refused to intervene on behalf of Martin Luther King, who was confined in a prison in Georgia, and when he refused to answer questions raised about whether or not he would include blacks in his cabinet. Jack said his refusal to part with Nixon earlier was a combination of stubbornness and his long-held belief that too-uniform black support of the Democrats had led them to take blacks for granted; leverage would come only when we had influence in both parties. I followed the logic of his thinking, but as a third-generation Democrat it pained me to see him cross over into alien and conservative territory.

His next major leap into politics took place in 1964. After seven years at Chock Full O'Nuts, he had grown restless and decided to resign in order to pursue both political and business opportunities. New York Governor Nelson Rockefeller, an aspiring presidential candidate, appointed him one of six national directors of his campaign, beginning a friendship that was to last until the end of Jack's life. Later, in February 1966,

No. 16 114

MOUNT OLIVE BAPTIST CHURCH
BUILDING FUND

9-12 1963 1-12/210

PAY TO THE ORDER OF B.B. Blaylock & A. Kinnon $10,000.

Ten Thousand DOLLARS

Jackie Robinson

Martin Luther King Jr.

CHEMICAL BANK NEW YORK TRUST COMPANY
633 THIRD AVENUE (41ST STREET)
NEW YORK

SEP 18 1963

⑁0210⑁0012⑁ 114⑁007268⑁

Dr. Martin Luther King asked Jack to head up a national fund-raising drive to rebuild the Mount Olive Baptist Church. He received substantial donations from Governor Nelson Rockefeller and William Black. This check is from the fund's account.

Rockefeller appointed Jack his special assistant for community affairs and a commissioner of boxing. Jack's joining Rockefeller was a risky move because he served completely at Rockefeller's pleasure, and because he took a significant cut in pay to do so. But, when he asked my opinion, I told him to follow his instincts. I wasn't just being magnanimous. I truly felt he had earned the right to do what he wanted to do. One difference it made between us at home was in his attitude about my paychecks: When I had gone back to work in the early 1960s, he had mostly ignored my $8,000 salary, treating it as one thing to tease me about. Now, as he shoved off into the murky waters of politics, he was happy to acknowledge any and all resources, including my contribution to the family coffers.

In 1965, at the invitation of Fritz Redlich, Dean of the Yale University Medical School, and Florence Wald, Dean of the School of Nursing, I accepted a joint appointment as Director of Nursing for the Connecticut Mental Health Center (CMHC) and Assistant Professor of Nursing. I spent the following seven years in this state-funded, Yale-operated facility, which offered a comprehensive range of services, research, and advanced clinical teaching. Medical Director Gerald Klerman, M.D., Associate Director of Nursing Nancy French, R.N., YSN Director of Psychiatric Nursing Retaugh Dumas, R.N., and I formed a skilled team of professionals dedicated to high standards of care, teaching, and research. We established new models and expanded roles for nurses, which put us in the forefront of psychiatric practice. It was my opportunity to attempt to apply much of what I learned at Einstein. While commuting to New Haven, I spent the quiet time planning my work and evaluating our progress at CMHC. On the way home, I would prepare to enter my family's life, more stimulated than if I had stayed there in my old role. My mother's presence helped to lessen the guilt about leaving home . . . not completely, but some. The children's adolescent years were fast approaching, and every now and again I was tempted to return home full-time, but I resisted.

ABOVE: *Jack campaigning with Richard Nixon in 1960. Jack believed with great conviction that political activism was essential to meaningful social change. He chose his man first and his party second. Choosing Nixon proved to be a mistake he regretted.* LEFT: *Jack campaigned for Hubert Humphrey in the 1968 presidential election. He spent many days on the road and in private discussion refining his ideas and preparing speeches. He was deeply disappointed by Humphrey's defeat.*

ABOVE: *Jack met Nelson Rockefeller in 1962 and was charmed by his apparent sincerity but was wary because there were no blacks in his administration. After a series of high-level meetings with black leaders that Jack organized, significant changes were instituted, including the appointment of blacks to high positions. In 1964 Jack became one of six national directors of Rockefeller's campaign. Jack's collaborator Alfred Duckett appears in the background.* ABOVE RIGHT: *Jack rejoices with Governor Rockefeller and Senator Jacob Javits, his campaign manager, when Rockefeller was re-elected in 1966.*

RIGHT: *In May 1963 Jack and Floyd Patterson went to Birmingham, Alabama, to join the protest movement led by Dr. Martin Luther King. After arriving in Birmingham, Jack and Floyd conferred with Ralph D. Abernathy (second from left) and Reverend King before addressing gatherings at two churches.* BELOW: *Jack often spoke at churches and other gathering places.*
OPPOSITE BELOW: *I was greatly pleased when Jack had the opportunity to share the stage with Eleanor Roosevelt on more than one occasion. I admired her spirited approach to life and identified with her determination to be a significant person in her own right.*

BELOW: *We were deeply affected by the stamina and courage of Southerners fighting racial discrimination. Jack listens as a young choir sings at a mass meeting in St. Augustine, Florida.*

RIGHT: *And he marched. On June 16, 1964, he joined marchers as they prepared to move toward St. Augustine's business district.*

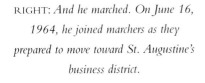

LEFT: *Jack confers with James Farmer, executive director of the Congress of Racial Equality, just before the beginning of a massive parade in San Francisco on July 12, 1964. Thousands of whites and Negroes used the parade to reject Senator Barry Goldwater's candidacy for the GOP presidential nomination. We had driven across the country with our children, and this convention was our final destination. The trip and the GOP convention stirred all of our senses.* OPPOSITE: *On another front on August 9, 1970, Jack joins the war on drugs at a block party in Harlem. He read a proclamation from Governor Nelson Rockefeller.*

32

Jazz

T H E   P E R F E C T   M E D I U M

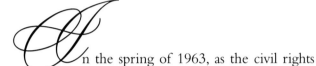

In the spring of 1963, as the civil rights movement intensified in the South, our need to find some way to help grew more urgent. In April, Martin Luther King and his deputies Wyatt T. Walker, Fred Shuttlesworth, Andy Young, and others led the Southern Christian Leadership Conference into Birmingham, Alabama, to begin a direct-action campaign against the city's pervasive racial discrimination. They boycotted downtown stores, conducted sit-ins at department stores, and finally marched on City Hall. As King anticipated, this provoked a furious, violent response from the city government; thousands were arrested. On Good Friday, King himself was put in solitary confinement. We watched, filled with outrage, as Bull Connor, Birmingham's infamous police commissioner, used snarling police dogs and high-pressure fire hoses to brutalize and try to break the spirit of the marchers. Other racists bombed homes and churches in Birmingham's black neighborhoods. Our anger overflowed when Governor George Wallace

ABOVE: *At the first jazz concert, Jack and I watch as members of the Herbie Mann Jazz Group instruct Sharon, thirteen, on flute and David, eleven, on drums. From left to right are Carlos Valdes, David, Sharon, Herbie Mann (with flute), and bass player Ben Tucker. The proceeds of the concert were donated to the NAACP, the Congress of Racial Equality, and the Southern Christian Leadership Conference.* OPPOSITE: *Oh happy day! Dollars from the jazz concert to be contributed to the civil rights movement.*

defied federal court orders to personally bar black students from enrolling at the University of Alabama. By June 12, 1963, when the murder of Medgar Evers in Jackson, Mississippi, struck us like a great blow, we were mobilizing our resources to help as best we could.

Jack had gone to Birmingham to meet with Dr. King and learned that what he needed most was bail money for the marchers who had already been jailed, and for those who would be arrested in future marches. We became preoccupied with the crisis and how to raise funds for that purpose. The idea struck us that our six-acre homesite—with its large, clear pond and hill that sloped down from the house to level ground in a way that formed a natural amphitheater—would be a lovely setting for an outdoor concert. Fortunately, Jack and I both were jazz enthusiasts and knew several musicians well. So, on the last Sunday in June, 1963, we produced the first Afternoon of Jazz on the lawn of our Stamford home. From the beginning, this event was designed, produced, and promoted by volunteers. For the inaugural concert, our family was joined by dear friends Marian and Arthur Logan, Bernice and Jack Gordon, and my brother Chuck Williams.

Marian had been a jazz singer in the thirties and forties, and Arthur was the personal physician of Duke Ellington. Their contacts gave us direct access to several recording artists. This small group did everything: We sold tickets, erected a stage, arranged artist transportation and equipment, greeted patrons, parked cars, and prepared and served a special luncheon for guests. We managed the crowd and stage, made speeches, introduced the artists, and cleaned up. My mother baked her delicious cakes for the raffle. We walked for miles, crisscrossing the six acres of our property, attending to this and that.

We were helped enormously by jazz great Billy Taylor; performer, composer, educator, and music critic George Simon; and radio personality Lee Murphy. With Marian, they formed a program committee that identified artists who were scheduled to be in the region; solicited participation; developed the program plan and used their professional status to give the event class and credibility. Nationally known recording artists Dave Brubeck, Dizzy Gillespie, the Adderleys, Joya Sherrill, and many others accepted our invitations to perform without payment and proved to be the most gracious and generous individuals that we ever encountered. The show for this inaugural event was outstanding. As *Life* magazine reported, we had "enough talent to stock a Newport Festival." To our great surprise, late in the afternoon a bus rolled into the driveway, and there was Duke Ellington and his band with vocalist Jimmie Rushing—what a treat that was.

We provided a musical feast for a racially mixed, harmonious audience of five hundred people. *Life* magazine referred to it as a "jam session for civil rights," and that it was. As the sun went down and the last guests departed, we all collapsed on the

living room floor, exhausted and overjoyed. We had $15,000 to send to Martin Luther King and the SCLC.

It was a splendid day and an auspicious beginning for the event that has become a jazz tradition. In 1995 in Norwalk, Connecticut, the "Afternoon of Jazz" attracted seven thousand jazz buffs, was run by three hundred volunteers, and was directed by Billy Taylor, produced by Robin Bell, and chaired by my daughter Sharon Robinson. Since 1973, the proceeds have benefited the Jackie Robinson Foundation, founded that year.

For more than three decades, the concert has brought people from all walks of life together. Families with picnic baskets and blankets have settled into their places by noon and stayed until sundown to hear Dizzy Gillespie, Herbie Mann, Dave Brubeck, Carol Sloan, Nat Adderley, Max Roach, George Shearing, Sarah Vaughn, Carmen McRae, Luther Henderson, Jimmie Owens, Ella Fitzgerald, Thelonious Monk, Clark Terry, Grady Tate, and regulars Joe Williams, Gerry Mulligan, Jimmy and Percy Heath, and the Billy Taylor Trio. More recently, young artists such as Noel Pointer, Sherry Winston, Wynton Marsalis, Terrence Blanchard, and Bobby Rodriguez have joined legendary greats Lionel Hampton, Milt Hinton, John Faddis, and others to continue this jazz tradition.

From the first concert to the latest, concert patrons have left telling us how much they enjoy participating in a peaceful assemblage of music lovers silently chanting for freedom. Jazz is the perfect medium to reflect life and the need people have to improvise and transcend barriers.

ABOVE LEFT: *Skitch Henderson performed, and Arthur Logan and I worked. I wore the same orange jazz dress with big pockets for many years to continue our good luck: We quietly and reverently acknowledge the fact that we have never been rained out.*

ABOVE: *This year the concert was weighted with sadness and outrage. The young civil rights activists Andy Goodman, James Chaney, and Mickey Schwerner were murdered on June 21, 1964, near Philadelphia, Mississippi. Proceeds from the concert were sent South to build a community center to commemorate their deeds and sacrifices. Left to right: Marian Logan, Jack, James Farmer, unknown, Robert and Carolyn Goodman (Andy's parents).*

RIGHT: *Billy Taylor, illustrious jazz pianist and most-cherished friend, became music director in the late sixties and continues to this day. His long-term commitment has enabled us to build this concert into a premier event.*

LEFT: *Great saxophonist Gerry Mulligan thrilled our audiences year after year. His devotion to our cause contributed handsomely to the growth of the jazz event.* ABOVE: *Young Joe Williams sings the blues. Joe, dear friend and valued "regular," has sung for us for over twenty years. On one occasion he sent us a huge check as well.* RIGHT: *This is Sarah Vaughn, the "Divine One." When she sang "Send in the Clowns" at twilight, our volunteer committee drew close in embrace to share our joy. Sarah not only contributed her enormous talent, but fueled our efforts with her generous spirit.*

ABOVE: *The master performer Dizzy Gillespie, steeped in jazz tradition and creating his own. He was a wonderful, playful longtime supporter of the Jackie Robinson Foundation.*
LEFT: *Ella Fitzgerald, the first lady of jazz, mesmerized the audience and drew them to her in awe and praise.*

ABOVE: *Wynton Marsalis, composer and performer of classical music and jazz, is one of the most exciting talents to emerge in years. He galvanizes young and old, volunteers and patrons.* RIGHT: *Max Roach drummed his way into our souls for years and years.*

RIGHT: *Putting the jazz concert together with an extraordinary group of professionals and volunteers brings a great sense of triumph. From 1980 to the present, Robin Bell Stevens has been our outstanding producer.*
BELOW: *Marian Logan chaired the gate committee from 1963 to 1985 along with Edith Elliott, Ellen Dickerson, and Sarah Cymrot. These women epitomized the backbone of the event and the heart of my circle of friends.*

33

Freedom National Bank

Freedom Bank expanded to include two branches in Brooklyn. This is the Flatbush office, which opened in 1984. Standing in front are Vice President George Bowman, President and CEO Sharnia Buford, and Senior Vice President Frank Hernandez.

We had long had connections to Harlem, the cultural and commercial capital of black America. During Jack's baseball years, our favorite restaurants there were Frank's, Jenny Lou's, and Mrs. Fraisier's. We gradually became jazz enthusiasts and frequented clubs in the area. Jack was fascinated by Harlem's history and potential and worried as many did about its future. Going back to the 1940s, Jack would occasionally meet Joe Louis, our "world champion for life," at the Hotel Theresa, or stop in to see Sugar Ray Robinson, the light heavyweight champ, at his restaurant on 7th Avenue. My favorite church in Harlem was Canaan Baptist, where the Reverend Wyatt T. Walker, one of Martin Luther King's chief deputies in the sixties, presided over a congregation of devoted worshipers and the most inspiring music in town. Jack made a point of serving on the Board of Managers of the Harlem YMCA on 135th Street from 1957 to 1969, where a building now bears his name. He had made the administrative offices of the famed Apollo Theater on 125th Street his favorite hangout, and spent time there with such friends as owner Bobby Schiffman, resident comedian Peter Long, and emcee Ralph Cooper. He had great respect for Manhattan Borough President Percy Sutton, a leader on every front, and Charlie Rangel, now the area's effective congressman, with whom he would discuss the political and economic developments affecting the community. In these hopeful times, when anything seemed possible, we both strongly identified with the area, although I'm sure we were considered newcomers.

In the early 1960s, Jack grew increasingly determined to find specific ways to help improve the lives of black people, and decided he would concentrate on stimulating economic development and political power, or, as he characterized it, the use of "the ballot and the buck." He considered a variety of proposals, but nothing got his full attention until Dunbar McLaurin, a Harlem businessman, approached him in 1963 with the idea of establishing a minority-owned-and-operated commercial bank in Harlem. McLaurin headed a group of entrepreneurs and activists who were ready to make the dream a reality. After some discussion, Jack signed on. Freedom National Bank was chartered in 1964 and through 1990 was the only African-American–owned and –operated com-

mercial bank in New York State. He became the first chairman of the board; William Hudgins, the president; the Honorable Herbert Evans, the treasurer; and Sam Pierce, the general counsel. Pioneering businesswoman Rose Morgan and other key community leaders formed the rest of the first board.

The bank's mission was to spur economic development and provide a full range of banking services to the Harlem community. Thousands of small investors contributed to the bank's early capitalization. Jack marveled as the lines of small investors formed on the sidewalk, and beamed with pride as he'd describe the procession.

In addition to its headquarters on 125th Street, Freedom subsequently opened two branch offices in Brooklyn, in Bedford-Stuyvesant and Flatbush. It peaked in performance in the mid-eighties and rose to the top of the minority bank charts, despite the fact that it was operating in the most difficult banking environment known to the industry and perennially struggled for profitability.

For many complex reasons, the always-vulnerable institution suffered periodic crises and Jack and the board would resort to a frenzy of activities to intervene. Jack wrote that his physical health was adversely affected by his worries about Freedom, and I listened as he talked endlessly at home about his investigations and the board's efforts to cope with the problems, many of which seemed to be managerial.

Participating in the leadership of Freedom and assisting in its phenomenal growth was one of Jack's most significant post-baseball achievements. It certainly gave him the most joy and the deepest pain. He was intensely aware that the success or failure of the bank had a heavy impact on first-time investors, small businesses, homeowners, and depositors. He knew its presence in Harlem was a catalyst for economic growth and a morale booster. The bank was the symbol of community control, self-sufficiency, black power, and black pride. It was concrete evidence of progress, hope for the future, rebuilding of a historically significant area. The emotional as well as business attachments to Freedom were immense.

I was serving on the board of directors when the comptroller of the currency first warned the board of the bank's failing condition and then, early one Monday morning in November 1990, they closed the doors.

For months after the closing, as I walked down the street filled with pain and disappointment, people would approach and often hug me, murmuring condolences, as if a family member had died. Indeed, our dream of equity, economic power, and social stability took a big hit when Freedom died. Freedom, or its successor bank, will rise again.

34

Born Too Soon

$\mathscr{I}$f there is any experience all parents share, it's the challenge of guiding their children through adolescence to adulthood. As Jack and I were establishing ourselves in new careers in the early sixties, we were also acutely aware that our children were struggling with all the physical and psychological changes the teen years bring. Their search for identity was complicated by Jack's fame as a baseball star and racial pioneer. In carving out new careers for ourselves, he and I were also presenting them with a new vision of ourselves and a wider, more challenging array of roles than just baseball star and housewife.

The challenge had a special impact on Jackie, who, as our first-born son and the bearer of Jack's name, had shared with us from infancy the bright glare of the public spotlight. Sharon and David, born four and six years later, also had to contend with the joy and complications of being the children of a famous parent, but somehow (I won't presume to preempt the memoirs they're contemplating) they acquired strengths Jackie didn't have.

Jackie was a kind and loving child, but, I realized in hindsight, very cautious and too dependent. It's possible that Jackie's behavior was affected by an undiagnosed learning disability; he was a very slow reader. Throughout elementary school we were able to help him a bit,

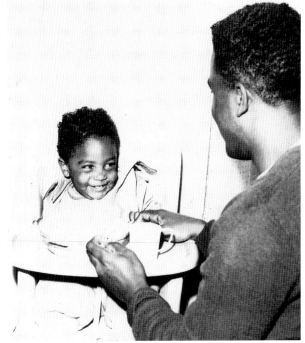
The flirtation.

and he particularly responded to the creative efforts of his fifth-grade teacher, Miss Carlucci, who tutored him and then often rewarded him with games of catch after school. But Jackie faltered when he entered his teen years and faced new experiences and responsibilities. As he moved from Dolan Junior High School on into Stamford High School, he found the atmosphere to be less supportive and more punitive. He became more confused and despairing. We sought professional help for him early on.

In 1962, at the suggestion of our friend the eminent psychologist Kenneth Clark, we sent him to The Stockbridge School, a boarding school in Interlaken, Massachusetts. Jackie was relieved to be out of Stamford and to have a fresh start. On a school field trip to Quebec he kept a diary, and in his summary of the trip he wrote, "The part I enjoyed most was the monastery. I find I have a clearer understanding of God." The beauty of Canada touched him, and in general the experiences at this school broadened his horizons. Unfortunately, at the end of the school year he was asked not to return because "he didn't fit in." Jackie returned to Stamford High, defeated, and in his frustration began to withdraw into a shell.

Looking back, I have no doubt that our deep love for our son prompted us to do what we could for him . . . but the painful truth was, we didn't know what to do in time to help. Jack felt completely baffled and helpless in the face of Jackie's growing aloofness. He had worked earnestly at being a good man and father, a man his son could be proud of, and he was tormented by Jackie's plight. Though I stayed close to Jackie, intervening at school, sitting and talking with him at all hours, arranging social and religious connections—we joined Jack and Jill, an organization that provided social outlets for black children and their families, and participated in the activities of the North Stamford Congregational Church, our neighborhood church—I didn't succeed in changing his direction either.

I did discover belatedly that I had unwittingly become a conduit for communications between the two Jacks, making it easier for them to stay apart. Jack would say to me, "Tell Jackie I think . . ." and Jackie would say, "Please tell Dad. . .". They became increasingly unable to talk with each other or embrace, as they had when he was younger; it was clear they longed to, in this tense period. They were not hostile, but paralyzed by some masculine defense and unable to bridge the gap between them.

We didn't realize Jackie had discovered what he thought was a solution to his problems until I ran into him walking down a main street in Stamford one day in early March 1964. With an air of confidence that I hadn't seen in him for a long time, he told me he was headed for the army recruitment office and said he had a lot of learning to do and needed discipline as well. He had been told the army offered both. Panicked, I persuaded him to sit down and talk. While I agreed with his assessment, I found myself pleading with him to consider other options. I would help, I vowed. But he was adamant, and so I went along numbly behind him to the recruitment office to listen to the pitch. I was convinced he was making a mistake, but I didn't know how to prevent it. Jackie was almost eighteen years old.

On March 30, 1964, he entered the infantry. He was as handsome in uniform as any soldier had ever been, and proud—he was going off to serve his country and become a man in the process. He was doing something positive, and his spirits were high. Our family gathered to see him off to basic training with heavy hearts, wanting to pull him back for one more urgent conversation or one more hug—but he was already on his way. Jack accepted this momentous change largely in silence, which was not surprising, given what his relationship with his son had become. What was he thinking? Probably that the military was a viable antidote to Jackie's confused adolescence—Jack was always inclined to put the best face on what seemed to be an insoluble problem.

To our great dismay, Jackie was sent to Vietnam after a few months in training. This transfer evoked my worst fears. Jackie was stunned as well, for he had enlisted actually hoping to be sent to Korea. In early 1964, Vietnam still seemed to be a skirmish, not a war. We prayed endlessly for his safety.

Tips from Dad.

RIGHT: *Jackie with Buffalo Bob and Clarabell from the "Howdy Doody Show," a creation of our friend Martin Stone.* BELOW: *A cherished moment with Jackie.* OPPOSITE ABOVE: *Fun together.* OPPOSITE BELOW: *Jack receiving the George W. Carver Award from publisher Frank Gannett as we proudly look on.*

Daddy receiving
George W. Carver award
from Frank Gannett
a millionaire publisher
1950

OPPOSITE: *Watching the ice skating and sharing a quiet moment at Grossinger's. Later, assembling a model plane.* ABOVE: *Jack and Jackie enjoying a pepper game at Vero Beach. The caption accompanying this press photo states, "The odds are against the youngster succeeding the father. . . . The boy's a lefty." It was precisely this kind of unwarranted negative forecast that Jackie had to endure.* ABOVE RIGHT: *Jackie (second row, far left) and his friend Peter Simon (first row, far right) at Camp Kokosing. We wanted Jackie to go, but we missed him so. Peter is now an outstanding photographer whose work is represented in this book.* BELOW RIGHT: *Jackie was the only Negro child on his Babe Ruth League team. He loved to play and seemed to hold his own except when razzed by unthinking spectator-parents.*

He wrote often to each of us. To Jack, his letters described the horrors of war and, ironically, now that they were miles apart, contained confidences a son could share only with his father. One such confidence revealed the birth of his only child, Sonya, and his conflict about marriage and parenting the lovely girl. At the time, his solution was to make Sonya the beneficiary of his GI insurance, and he asked us to support her mother when needed. To me he wrote about troop movements as his squad, the First Tank Battalion, moved from place to place, mostly to explain how mail was being forwarded or delayed. He would ask me to help in practical matters, like saving the money he sent home monthly or getting the supplies he needed. To David and Sharon he offered advice and counsel, big-brother style, and they were happy to hear anything from him. There was something reassuring about the exchange of letters. It reaffirmed the ties between Jackie and each of us. And it was a declaration that life had to go on with some semblance of normalcy even if one of us was in great danger. The need to be resilient was a challenge we'd all have to meet again and again in the next few years.

"Why do we have a commitment in Vietnam? I'll *tell* you why we have a commitment in Vietnam."

Jackie sent me a copy of this New Yorker *cartoon, which he captioned, "U.S. College Kids," adding, "A* man *got killed last week in my company who was younger than I am." Drawing by Donald Reilly; © 1965, 1993. The New Yorker Magazine, Inc.*

In one sense, Jackie's expectations of the army were fulfilled: He got the discipline he wanted. But the learning was far more painful than he had bargained for. Mired in battle, with his fellow soldiers and friends falling around him, Jackie was angered by the antiwar protests at home. He wrote me that he felt undermined by those "college kids" and "draft dodgers" who made U.S. soldiers feel denigrated and that they were willing dupes of our government. He sent this cartoon in the letter to dramatize his feelings.

But I suspect that part of his anger reflected his own doubts about the war, doubts provoked by the reality of the bloodshed in Vietnam. His letters mentioned the killing of innocent women and children. He described battle as "like shooting at ghosts." In one letter to Jack he wrote that some U.S. soldiers had killed a sniper, tied his body to the front of their jeep "like a deer," and driven through a village with a loudspeaker and a interpreter, warning the inhabitants that this is what would happen to all Viet Cong and their supporters. He said it was a horrible sight. The atrocities on our side stunned him.

On November 19, 1965, one day after his nineteenth birthday, Jackie suffered shrapnel wounds in the hip in an explosion that killed two men standing next to him. He was devastated by the loss, but never mentioned his own fear of death. On March 25, 1966, he received the Purple Heart and the Vietnam Defense Campaign Medal. His tour in Vietnam was almost over. He was given an honorable discharge in

1967 and was sent home spiritless, wounded in body and soul, cynical, afraid—and, worst of all, though we didn't know it at the time, a drug addict.

For a year after his discharge, Jackie, Jr., seemed lost, unable to hold a job, unable to settle in Stamford or elsewhere. We were mystified. Then, in early April 1968, he was arrested in Stamford on drug and weapons charges. Jack and I hit bottom. As we left the jail, Jack walked in front of me toward the waiting reporters. His stance was dignified, but his head was slightly bowed . . . heavy, it seemed. He made a simple statement, essentially holding himself responsible for Jackie's troubles, and finished by saying, "God is testing me." I said nothing; I could hardly see what was in front of me. Later, I arranged for Jackie to be admitted to Yale New Haven Hospital, where my most helpful colleague Dr. Herbert Kleber took over at least for a brief period.

Jackie's arrest and hospitalization inaugurated a period in which a series of tragedies touched us personally and made 1968 one of the worst years in our lives. Martin Luther King was assassinated in April, his death provoking riots in more than one hundred cities: We went from Jackie's hospital room to the funeral in Atlanta. Robert Kennedy would be assassinated in June, reinforcing the national sense of danger and sadness. And within our family, our dear Mallie Robinson died quietly in her garden in Pasadena on May 21. Jack went home to bury this wonderful woman, the wellspring of his being. Adding to our sudden sense of being star-crossed, Sharon made an unfortunate marriage, which soon failed. The combination of forces and happenings made me feel like "I Couldn't Hear Nobody Pray," a spiritual that says, "O, 'way down yonder by myself, an' I couldn't hear nobody pray."

Jackie, Jr., was fortunate: At his trial he was given a choice between jail and rehabilitation. He chose the latter, and was sent to the Daytop Rehabilitation Program in Seymour, Connecticut. Daytop is a residential community staffed by former addicts, which utilizes a group setting to emphasize personal responsibility. Jackie stayed there for almost three years, recovering from his addiction, and also regaining a positive sense of himself. After completing the program, he would become a Daytop counselor and inspirational speaker before school and community groups. Jack, proud and relieved, occasionally joined in his public presentations. In fact, we were all ecstatic over Jackie's progress, even while we were uncertain about how far the recovery would go. He came home for visits, sent cards, resumed his place in the family. He brought his daughter, Sonya, for visits, caring for her with great tenderness. The resolution of his difficult years seemed fragile to me, but I kept my doubts to myself. It was like believing in the resurrection.

We felt so grateful to the Daytop community that we held a picnic at our home to say "thanks" and to get to know them better. It was a joyous day, bright and sunny, and filled with good will and hope. At the end, as the guests were departing, Jack extended his hand to Jackie, and Jackie brushed it aside and gave him a big hug. Jack's eyes filled with tears—he had his son back.

By the time Jackie returned from Vietnam, I had already begun to wonder if he had been born too soon. It was just a notion, a mother's seeking to understand the forces that had shaped her child's life. As our firstborn, he had been born before we understood the stress celebrity status could have on families; born before a true understanding of learning problems was widespread; born before the spread of drugs forced greater drug education efforts for parents and their children; born before the ravages of our involvement in Vietnam on the soldiers sent there were even hinted at.

All of this was not an intellectual formulation, but a parent's feeling, perhaps a parent's way of mitigating guilt. Whatever its truth, by 1971 we all felt that Jackie's troubles seemed to be in the past. His future seemed brighter.

Roberta Flack returned to the jazz concert year after year. On June 27, 1971, in response to a wish Jackie had made before his death, she hesitantly took center stage and sang her way into our tormented hearts. She was my special blessing on that fateful day.

We decided to make a sizable contribution to Daytop by dedicating the 1971 "Afternoon of Jazz" concert to them and donating all proceeds to the program. Jackie was delighted and joined our volunteer committee. He took the lead in contacting artists, starting with his favorite, Roberta Flack. The concert was scheduled for the last Sunday in June.

Jackie didn't live to see the day. On June 17, 1971, he was killed in an automobile accident while driving home from New Haven on the Merritt Parkway. We staged the concert in his honor on the sloping hill behind our house, and Roberta Flack sang as long as she could bear to. Reverend Jesse Jackson spoke eloquently and held a short prayer service in our bedroom, which I reluctantly attended. I put on a long African dress and wandered through the audience in a daze, on the edge of madness (as I imagined it to be). Almost no one approached me.

Seeking an anchor to ward off the distress, I drifted down the hill to the stage and sat on the piano bench next to my dear friend Billy Taylor. He just moved over and continued playing. He knew me well enough to know that music brought me the only solace I could accept. And then I suddenly left the stage and retreated up the hill toward the house. David, who had been watching over me, met me halfway and took my hand, and we ran together crying hard in flight. In that moment I felt we had gained so much in life, and lost it all when we lost our Jackie.

At Jackie's funeral held at Antioch Baptist Church, my mother's church in Brooklyn, the Daytop choir sang, and David read a tribute called "The Baptism" that he had composed in Jackie's honor. In a strong voice filled with pain, he spoke for all of us.

THE BAPTISM

And he climbed high on the cliffs above the sea and stripped bare his shoulders, and raised his arms to the water, crying "I am a man, I live and breathe and bleed as a man. Give me my freedom so that I might dance naked in the moonlight and laugh with the stars as they play amongst the darkness in the sky and roll in the grass and drink the warmth of the sun and feel it sweet within my body. Give me my freedom so that I might fly." But the armies of the sea continued to war with the beach, and the wind raced through the giants of stones which guard the coast and its howl mocked his cries, and the man fell to his knees and wept.

Then he rose and journeyed down the mountain to the valley and came upon a village. When the people saw him they scorned him for his naked shoulders and wild eyes and again he cried "I am a man, and I seek the means of my freedom." But the people laughed at him saying, "We see no chains on your arms, no weight on your feet. Go, you are free, fly, fly." And they called him mad and drove him from their village. But his soul wept, for it knew the weight of chains, and tears fell like tiny stones into the vast well of his loneliness and his heart was empty as a giant hall is empty after a feast.

And the man journeyed on until he came to the banks of a stream, and his eyes, red as the gladiator's sword, strained, for he saw an image dance across the stillness of that water and he recognized the figure though his eyes were now sunken with hunger, and his skin drawn tight around his body, and he stood fixed above the water's edge and began to weep, not from sorrow but from joy, for he saw beauty in the water and he removed his clothing and stood naked before the world, and he rose to his full height and smiled as the sun kissed his body, and he moved to meet with the figure in the water, and the stream made love to his body, and his soul cried with the ecstasy of being one, and he sent the water flying up like a shower of diamonds to the sky, and he laughed, for he felt the strength of the stream flowing through his veins, and he cried, "I am a man," and the majesty of his voice echoed off the mountaintops and was heard above the roar of the sea and the howl of the wind, and he was free!

David expressed his grief this way, and W. E. B. Du Bois expressed my unspoken anguish in other words, from "Of the Passing of the First-Born" in The Souls of Black Folk:

Within the Veil was he born, said I; and there within shall he live,—a Negro and a Negro's son. Holding in that little head—ah, bitterly!—the unbowed pride of a hunted race, clinging with that tiny dimpled hand—ah, wearily!— to a hope not hopeless but unhopeful, and seeing with those bright wondering eyes that peer into my soul a land whose freedom is to us a mockery and whose liberty a lie. I saw the shadow of the Veil as it passed over my baby, I saw the cold city towering above the blood-red land. I held my face beside his little cheek, showed him the star-children and the twinkling lights as they began to flash, and stilled with an even-song the unvoiced terror of my life.

OPPOSITE: *Private Jackie Robinson, Jr.*
OPPOSITE LEFT: *Jackie was home on leave at the end of 1965 before going to Vietnam. He was in great shape, and proud, but apprehensive.*

ABOVE: *Jackie became an inspirational speaker for Daytop and was occasionally joined by his proud father.*
LEFT: *Postwar and post-rehab at Daytop, we held a picnic for Daytop members at our Stamford home. After three years Jackie (here, he and David flank a member) was robust and hopeful.*

Suddenly Jackie was gone.
On June 22, 1971, Jack holds me and
Sharon's husband Joe Mitchell
comforts her following Jackie's funeral at
New York's Antioch Baptist
Church. David read "The Baptism."
Our only solace was that Jackie was free
at last. OPPOSITE: The concert
dedicated to Jackie and Daytop: Daytop
director Kenny Williams and
Reverend Jesse Jackson helped us through
that excruciatingly painful day.

206

Making It Home

In the last years of his life Jack finally found the business opportunity he had been searching for since leaving baseball a decade earlier. Backed by a small group of investors organized by his lawyer and loyal friend, Marty Edelman, Jack established the Jackie Robinson Construction Company to build housing for families with low and moderate incomes. It was a prospect that shored up his failing health and fueled his courageous heart. With a contract from the New York State Urban Development Corporation and a joint-venture agreement with Halpern Building Corporation, the new company in 1970 broke ground for Whitney Young Manor, a 197-unit apartment development in Yonkers, New York.

Jack set up an office in Fort Lee, New Jersey, near that of one of the company's investors, Richard Cohen (the other investor was Mickey Weissman). His support group included Merlyn White, his strong executive assistant; Kiah Sayles, his aide-de-camp; and Joel Halpern, the owner of Halpern Building Corp. They surrounded him with skilled help and personal loyalty that knew no bounds. They were his final blessing. Marty was extraordinarily supportive and vigilant, and his devotion helped sustain Jack's will to achieve and capacity to function. Each night at about 10 P.M. Marty would call Jack to review the day's events and make plans. I felt the calls were a tender way for a friend to ease his mentor into a quiet night of rest, and though I didn't know Marty at the time, I loved him for it.

Jack had a mild heart attack in 1968, and then another in 1970. His eyesight was failing, and he silently endured extreme pain in his legs. The new business helped Jack's morale immensely, but it could not prevent physical deterioration. And yet he kept going at his usual relentless pace. On one day in September 1971, for example, Jack played nine holes in a charity golf tournament in Westchester County, New York, taking time after play had finished to kibitz with spectators in the gallery. Then, after gathering up several sandwiches, we hopped in the car and drove five hours to Washington, D.C., to be in attendance as Sharon received her nurse's cap at Howard University. We were both so proud. This was important to our daughter, and Jack's love for her would not let him think of missing it. He was extremely tired, but he stayed after the ceremony to sign autographs for Sharon's classmates who surrounded him. This was the way Jack had always lived his life. We didn't talk about the shadow hovering over us, we maintained our individual schedules as best we could, and we squeezed in doctor's

"Salute to the Champs" 1970: Having fun with Joe Louis, Joe Frasier, and Muhammad Ali. OPPOSITE: *Jack participates in the groundbreaking ceremony for Whitney Young Manor, accompanied by New York Urban Development Corporation officials William Hayden and James Robinson.*

visits as necessary. It was like being in a race . . . a race with death.

One evening in early 1972, Jack arrived home visibly shaken. He had almost hit a car on the parkway: The near-miss forced him to finally admit that he had completely lost all peripheral vision. I immediately hired a chauffeur. But Jack, to show his disdain for the arrangement, rode up front with the driver and loudly played the all-news radio station WINS from Stamford to Fort Lee and back to curtail any attempts at conversation. Given his lifelong passion to be self-sufficient and his love of driving, his need for a chauffeur was an unmistakable indication of his growing dependency on others, and he hated it. When he grumbled about his driver, I just smiled to myself. I was relieved that he wasn't driving—and that I wasn't the chauffeur.

In the summer of 1972 it occurred to me that I should assemble the family to take

RIGHT: *Old soldiers never die;*
they fight until the end. Jack with
Commissioner Bowie Kuhn, always a
strong supporter, as Jack throws out the
first ball at the 1972 World Series.
BELOW: *Roy Campanella's,*
Sandy Koufax's, and Jack's numbers
were retired in Dodgers Stadium in June
1972. Appearing on the field with
Jack were Campy (with his aide), Sandy
Koufax in uniform, National League
President Charles Feeney, Commissioner
Bowie Kuhn, and owner/president
Peter O'Malley.

ABOVE: *Jack was honored at the 1972 World Series in Riverfront Stadium, Cincinnati. He made a passionate statement about his longing to see a black manager in the majors. He did not live to see the day. Shown with him are Commissioner Bowie Kuhn, friend Patricia Hammock, David, Sharon (behind Jack), Charles Feeney, Peter O'Malley, and teammates Joe Black and Larry Doby.*

LEFT: *On December 6, 1971,* Sport Magazine *celebrated its twenty-fifth anniversary with a luncheon for top performers at Mamma Leone's restaurant, where Jack was honored. Among the attendees were basketball great Bill Russell, who towered over Jack and gave him a bear hug. This award-winning photo shows Jack's emotional response.*

OPPOSITE: *As we assembled in August 1972 for this photo, Jack whispered, "the last hurrah"* —a prophetic statement. ABOVE: *Jack died on October 23, 1972. Former teammates and friends attend his funeral on October 27 at Riverside Church. Shown outside the church are (left to right) Joe Black, Roy Wilkins, one-time Dodger Ralph Branca, former Yankee Elston Howard, and Don Newcombe. In the background are Larry Doby and Ernie Banks.*
RIGHT: *My son David and Reverend Jesse Jackson assist me as we leave Riverside Church.*
I have no comforting perspective on the moment, except to understand that I had to descend into the depths of grief, unrestrained, before I could rise again and step back into living. The loss felt unbearable.

a trip with Jack. You might call it a premonition. So, our old friend Marian Logan, my mother, Sharon, David, Jack, and I went to a lovely condo in Dragon's Bay, Jamaica, for a week. Through the years Jamaica had been our favorite place to be. Marty secured the location and made all of the arrangements. We had an excellent cook and housekeepers so we were totally free to live on the beach. Beaches in general held little attraction for Jack, but we persuaded him that the seawater would be good for his legs. How grateful I am for that trip. It gave us time together in close quarters to begin to heal from the loss of Jackie and to strengthen the bonds between us. David, who had dropped out of Stanford University after Jackie's death and was working in New York, had become a source of strength for Jack, going to meetings with him and generally giving his father someone acceptable to lean on. In Jamaica David acted as Jack's aide and protector on trips to and from the beach. Sharon, who adored her father and had been in Washington at Howard University, had time to be closer. In the evenings we played games and talked quietly in pairs. The week was a gift.

Our family gathered one other time, on October 15, 1972, when Jack was honored before the start of the second game of the World Series between the Reds and the Pirates at Riverfront Stadium, Cincinnati. When *Sepia* magazine asked all of us to pose for a formal family picture, Jack murmured, "the last hurrah." I winced. At the game he was seated with Commissioner Bowie Kuhn, sportswriter Joe Reichler, Peter O'Malley, Joe Black, and Larry Doby and was surrounded by his former teammates and opponents. The game of life was almost over for Jack, but he had his final say as he accepted the honors of the day. In a voice quavering with emotion, he said, "I'd like to live to see a black manager, I'd like to live to see the day when there is a black man coaching at third base." At the airport on the way home he seemed especially weary. I wondered if he felt his farewell statement to baseball had fallen on deaf ears. Old soldiers never never ever give up.

On October 22, 1972, while we were watching a football game together on television, Jack suddenly got up and turned the TV off, saying he had detected a flash in his good eye. Such bright flashes often signaled the rupture of a small blood vessel in the eye. A sickening thought raced between us. Without discussion, we called his doctor and scheduled an early-morning appointment. The devastating prognosis of blindness lingered in the air that night as we fell asleep in a tight embrace. Early the next morning, I was in the kitchen preparing breakfast, and Jack was dressing for the 9 A.M. appointment in New York. I looked up, and Jack was rushing down the hallway from the bedroom to the kitchen, obviously headed for me. So I ran to him. He put his arms around me, said, "I love you," and just dropped to the floor.

As I swiftly moved to deal with the emergency, I had a vague feeling that in a fantasy of "what would I do if . . . ," I had rehearsed for this moment more than once. As I did what I could, I struggled to stay out of the mental abyss I sensed overcoming me, until help arrived. Our neighbor and friend Sidney Kweskin arrived, and then and only then did I cry and cry. My dearest Jack, my giant, had been struck down, striving to live and loving to the very end.

Within a few weeks, I conjured up a thought that never mitigated the sense of loss, but had only to do with my protective feeling: He made it home . . . safe.

Our loved ones followed him too rapidly for us to comprehend. My mother died in April 1973, and our old friend dear Arthur Logan, in November 1973.

As the survivors—David, Sharon, and I—moved close to each other, on 93rd and 94th Streets in Manhattan, we moved even closer in a spiritual sense. We were filled with pain, but glory also, for we had loved and joined a great man, dear father, and precious husband, on a triumphant journey transcending and sustaining hope all the way.

FROM THE EULOGY BY REVEREND JESSE JACKSON AT THE FUNERAL OF JACKIE ROBINSON

Jackie's body was a temple of God, an instrument of peace that had no commitment to the idle gods of fame and materialism and empty awards and cheap trophies. . . .

Jackie, as a figure in history, was a rock in the water, hitting concentric circles and ripples of new possibility. Jackie, as a co-partner with God, was a balm in Gilead, in America, in Ebbets Field. . . .

When Jackie took the field, something within us reminded us of our birthright to be free. And somebody without reminded us that it could be attained. There was strength and pride and power when the big rock hit the water, and concentric circles came forth and ripples of new possibility spread throughout this nation. . . .

He didn't integrate baseball for himself. He infiltrated baseball for all of us, seeking and looking for more oxygen for black survival, and looking for new possibility. . . .

His feet on the baseball diamond made it more than a sport, a narrative of achievement more than a game. For many of us . . . it was a gift, of new expectations, on that dash. . . .

He helped us to ascend from misery, to hope, on the muscles of his arms, and the meaning of his life. With Rachel, he made a covenant, where he realized that to live is to suffer, but to survive is to find meaning in that suffering. Today we can raise our hands and say Hallelujah. . . .

In his last dash, Jackie stole home. Pain, misery, and travail have lost. Jackie is saved. His enemies can leave him alone. His body will rest, but his spirit and his mind and his impact are perpetual and as affixed to human progress as are the stars in the heavens, the shine in the sun and the glow in the moon. This mind, this mission, could not be held down by a grave. . . .

No grave can hold this body down. It belongs to the ages, and all of us are better off because the temple of God, the man with convictions, the man with a mission, passed this way.

OPPOSITE LEFT ABOVE: *David (third from left) and Jesse Jackson (fourth from left) join other mourners in paying final respects in Brooklyn. To the right are my mother, Zellee, my brother Chuck, and civil rights activist Bayard Rustin.*
OPPOSITE LEFT BELOW: *Among the many mourners were Jack's dear friend and schoolmate Ray Bartlett, Lacy Covington, David, Jesse Jackson, Joe Mitchell, Zellee Isum, Chuck Williams, and Bayard Rustin. I couldn't bear to see the burial and remained in the car. My last visual memory of Jack was of the vibrant living person.*
Active Pallbearers:
Bill Russell, Larry Doby, Monte Irvin, Martin Edelman, Jim Gilliam, Don Newcombe, Arthur Logan, Ralph Branca, Pee Wee Reese, Ray Bartlett, Joe Black
Honorary Pallbearers:
Willie Mays, Joe Louis, Nelson Rockefeller, Richard Cohen, Willie Stargell, Peter Long, Roy Campanella, A. Philip Randolph, Bayard Rustin, Martin Stone, Robert Boyd, Frank Schiffman, Roy Wilkins, Elston Howard, Kiah Sayles
OPPOSITE RIGHT: *Jack's funeral cortege headed for Cypress Hills Cemetery in Brooklyn by way of Harlem and Bedford-Stuyvesant. The drama captured here is enhanced by the symbolic significance of a man saying farewell with the black power salute.* LEFT: *Making it home . . . safe.*

36

Walk On

David, Sharon, and I—The Survivors—strolling through the campus of Yale University, happy to be together, happy to be alive. We were still recovering from the most painful period of our lives. We lost Jackie in '71, Jack in '72, Zellee in '73, and Arthur Logan in '73. This is my favorite picture of the three of us.

Within weeks of Jack's death, I resigned, with regret, from Yale University and, with Marty's help and the investors' consent, became the president of Jack's company. My partners, Richard Cohen and Mickey Weissman, helped me set up an office in their conference room at 280 Park Avenue in New York City, and Merlyn White, Jack's loyal assistant, came to work for me. I immediately decided we didn't have the capital or expertise to be a construction company, as Jack had envisioned. But we did have the resources to be a real estate development company, to get the contracts and the financing that would give us the responsibility to see to it that projects got built. We became the Jackie Robinson Development Corporation (JRDC) and established a joint venture with the Halpern Building Corporation to build Whitney Young Manor in Yonkers, as Jack had earlier contracted for.

Putting the company together forced me to concentrate and act on my own behalf, because our family's financial survival and the future of the company was at stake. But once that initial emergency passed, my grief came flooding to the surface. It was visceral as well as mental: I literally felt I had a hole in my abdomen and would walk around with my hands covering my stomach. I felt exposed and raw; I couldn't yet absorb the deaths of the two most important men in my life.

Marty would come to my home and to the office and diagram for me the fundamentals of development, corporate structures, and limited partnerships, while I struggled to concentrate so I could provide responsible leadership for the company. Because my attention span was so fractured by the trauma I had been through, he patiently repeated the lessons over and over again. In time, it became easier to push myself to perform. I think I realized there was no place for me to hide. I needed to walk on.

Together the Jackie Robinson Development Corporation and Halpern Building Corporation eventually built and managed 1,300 units of low- and moderate-income housing in Yonkers, Brooklyn, and Manhattan under the sponsorship of the New York State Urban Development Corporation. Using the skills I had developed at Yale, I created the methods and materials that allowed us to expand into training property managers, primarily for New York City and New York State housing agencies. Within a short time, the company stabilized, and I felt as though I had rescued Jack's final dream and secured my own future.

In 1973, after the business was underway, my brother Chuck Williams, Marty Edel-

LEFT: *Edgar Robinson, Jack's eldest brother, was the sweet one, deeply religious and warm. He was an extraordinary speed skater and bike rider. He outlived Jack by eighteen years.*
BELOW: *For me "walking on" meant going back to work, living alone, and also managing a large house without fear. My granddaughter Susan and I are cutting the lawn on our tractor.*

BELOW: *Marty Edelman, my lawyer, tutor, and dear friend, prepares me for the business world.*

man, and Franklin Williams met with me to consider how we could create a "living memorial" to Jack. Each of us had been inspired by Jack's legacy: his activism, courage, and enduring commitment to social justice. We were determined to find a way to perpetuate that legacy for future generations. Chuck represented the family interests, Marty provided the legal expertise, Franklin provided the meeting space and initial corporate contacts, and I provided the salary for our first employee. We incorporated as the Jackie Robinson Foundation (JRF), a public, not-for-profit national organization which would provide education and leadership development opportunities principally for minority youth with strong capabilities and limited financial resources. For at least two years our paid "staff" consisted solely of Ruth Hunt. She helped hold the organization together from a small cubicle at the Phelps Stokes Fund. In 1977 Chesebrough-Pond's, Inc., and their extraordinary CEO, Ralph Ward, gave us the funds to award our first two scholarships and helped us devise our program model, which includes tuition, summer jobs, internships, and mentoring. Along with other companies, Chesebrough-Pond's' own participation has not only continued, but grown in the two decades since.

Under the leadership of our two presidents, first, Jerry Lewis, and now, Betty Adams, we've sent almost four hundred students to colleges throughout the country backed by $20,000 awards and a range of vital support services. In 1995 there were 129 Jackie Robinson Scholars matriculating in fifty-nine colleges and universities in twenty states. We have an impressive ninety-percent graduation rate, and almost all graduates become involved in our Alumni Association, through which they can "give back" in a variety of ways. These talented young adults find employment or enter graduate and professional schools for further training. We proudly share in their achievements and the contributions they make to the well-being of the communities they reside in.

The program has fulfilled the vision that Chuck, Marty, Franklin, and I started with in those difficult days after Jack's death. Out of that great loss we've gained an extended family of individuals who stand proudly on Jack's shoulders and give life to his legacy.

As we established our mission and goals, this group and our work together enabled me to rise up from the depths of profound grief and move on. In 1946, at the start of what author Jules Tygiel called the "Great Experiment," Jack and I could not have begun to envision such triumph and spreading of achievement based primarily on an indomitable spirit and his gifts to humankind.

As I reflect on my life, I think of it as a creative struggle, and I share the convictions of the great abolitionist Frederick Douglass, who, in a speech made in New York on August 4, 1857, said, "If there is no struggle there is no progress." I am one of the fortunate ones granted a mission at the age of twenty-three, a great partner, and the spirit to prevail.

LEFT: *I'm talking to Reverend Wyatt T. Walker, pastor of Canaan Baptist Church, and a civil rights and community leader for decades. Reverend Walker and his church are pioneering sponsors of low- and moderate-income housing and programs for the elderly in Harlem. Here we are discussing Canaan House (in rear), constructed by JRDC and sponsored by the church.*

OPPOSITE LEFT: *My work as president of the Jackie Robinson Development Corporation. Whitney Young Manor in Yonkers was the first housing development my company completed. Jack and I shared a dream of quality living for every family, so this building had special significance for me. On the day of the dedication I posed with County Executive Alfred Del Bello. Keeping the project well maintained was the theme of the day: Hence, brooms were the symbol.*

OPPOSITE RIGHT: *It was such a thrill to see children playing in the new city-built recreational facility next to the Whitney Young Manor development.*

RIGHT: *"Walking on" meant leaning just a little on my handsome and loving brother Chuck, who was a vice president of Schenley's Industries. He consistently walked through all of life's paths with me until November 11, 1994. I will miss him always.*

37

The Legacy

From my many encounters with people on the street, on the bus, and everywhere I travel, I feel that the legacy of Jackie Robinson has been carried forward in the hearts of the men and women whose lives he touched. From the stories they tell me, I can see that they consciously try to remember and live by his values. They encourage me.

Also, a significant number of organizations, programs, schools, parks, community centers, and other facilities bearing his name make a special effort to form a living tribute; many of their programs are designed in emulation of their hero. Our family and the Jackie Robinson Foundation concretely perpetuate his memory and the thrust of his life's work in other ways. For example, as we strengthen young people by providing education and leadership opportunities, we are giving them the tools to remain hopeful and build their self-esteem, as well as the opportunity to lead meaningful lives and give back to others.

These photographs represent just a few of the participants in Jackie Robinson Foundation activities. The impact of our work can be seen in the bright faces, brilliant work, and community service provided by Jackie Robinson Scholars and alumni.

OPPOSITE: *Bill Cosby, great performer and humanitarian, President and C.E.O. Betty Adams, and Program Director Emma Robeson surrounded by Jackie Robinson Scholars attending our annual networking weekend. Bill Cosby, a longtime supporter, personifies the strengths of the foundation. We attract talented people who make long-term commitments to youth.* RIGHT: *Chuck Williams, surrounded by the Robinson and Williams families (left to right): Son Dr. Charles Williams III, daughter Rhoda Alexander, son Dr. Kirk Williams, grandson Louis Alexander, David Robinson and his wife, Ruti, my grandchildren Sonya, Jesse, Li, and Sherita, and Sharon Robinson. On this night Chuck received the JRF Founders Award. Absent are my granddaughters Ayo and Faith Robinson, Susan Thomas, and Rachel Robinson II, and grandson Howard Eaton. The family as the ideal structure for growth is another concept vital to JRF's program model.*

Peter O'Malley, President of the Los Angeles Dodgers and major supporter of the Jackie Robinson Foundation. Peter and I enjoy a close friendship. We have worked to put the tensions between Jack and Peter's father, Walter, behind us.

JACKIE ROBINSON FOUNDATION BOARD OF DIRECTORS

mong my most cherished child-hood memories are the times when my father took me to New York City. The father-daughter excursions began after he retired from baseball, when I was about seven years old, and continued through-out his life. I would have my father's full attention for that whole day.

We would begin at his Chock Full O'Nuts office, where his employees made a big fuss over me and shared favorite stories from the Brooklyn Dodgers days. It would end with a shopping spree in the wholesale clothing district of Manhattan. At designer Joseph Love's shop, Dad and Mr. Love talked baseball and politics while I was escorted around the factory and allowed to pick glorious dresses from his upcom-ing collection. Satisfied with my box of dresses, we would proceed to a lingerie house where Dad and I picked out beautiful negligees for my mother.

As a child it was difficult to reconcile Jackie Robinson, famous baseball player, with my Dad. On one level, I acknowledged that they were the same. On another, it was important for me to keep them separate.

My world was full of reminders of Dad's importance: the speaking engagements, the fact that family outings were never private, the tributes, invi-tations, and honors were the evidence. The trophy room on the lower level of our house was devoted to Dad's plaques, trophies, and prized baseball mem-orabilia. As a family we were featured on the covers of *Look*, *Ebony*, *Sepia*, and *Jet* magazines and interviewed on Edward R. Murrow's television talk show in the fifties.

My parents became the most closely watched and admired couple in the black community, my father an icon. While the tendency is to confine their accomplishments to the world of professional baseball, in reality my parents were social engineers. The challenge to integrate major-league baseball was only the first of many stages in their support of the civil rights movement. In fact, Dad continued to serve as a vehicle for change until the day he died.

The high visibility that traced my parents' steps brought with it responsibility, high expectations, and pressures that made normal adolescent development especially difficult. Mom and Dad did try to shelter us and compensate for the fact that we shared them with the world. They chose to raise us in the country, took us on lots of family vacations, and kept us involved in their mission. Ultimately, the price we paid for social pioneering was high. David and I lost our brother in a car accident at the age of twenty-four. A year later, our father died of a heart attack at fifty-three, leaving us with a legacy of great accomplishment and a lifetime of memories.

While I have struggled to define his legacy, I have arrived at a definition of service and clearly see how my mother, my brother, and I—along with countless others—carry forth the mission with confidence. Institutions have been built that bear the name of Jackie Robinson, we work in our foundation, which provides financial support to hundreds of Jackie Robinson Scholars, and my brothers and I have produced another fine generation of Robinsons.

Today, Mom, David, and I stand tall as survivors with strength and a rich sense of purpose. Mom transferred the knowledge and skills acquired as a psychiatric nurse into a successful business career and

founded the Jackie Robinson Foundation. David has found fulfillment in his work and life in East Africa. And I satisfy my passion for excellence as a mother, nurse-midwife, and teacher. While we have chosen very different places to be of service, our commitment to our people, sensitivity to social change, and devotion to family is consistent.

The children that my brothers and I have produced will never sit on their grandfather's lap, hear his stories, or know his protectiveness. Yet they have embraced his competitive spirit, commitment, and determination, and have come to know of Jackie Robinson from the misty eyes of others.

As an adult, I am able to appreciate Jackie Robinson as a man, American icon, husband, and father—however, it is the father that I miss, deeply love, and cannot replace.

Sharon Robinson is a graduate of Howard and Columbia Universities, a practicing nurse-midwife, and Assistant Clinical Professor at the Yale School of Nursing. She is married to Molver Fieffe and is the proud mother of Jesse Martin Robinson Simms.

The house that my parents built, in which I grew up, had great stones as its foundation and an interior paneled in polished woods. On three sides forests extended for miles, and two large lakes dominated the topography. This home was not isolated from the world, but was rather a world unto itself, from which I went daily into the other worlds beyond. Less than twenty minutes' drive from our house there were various private clubs that would not admit me due to my race, yet at home my mother would make up marvelous bedtime stories for me of my heroic participation as a knight in King Arthur's Court.

In the early 1960s black people were trying to remember our past and deal with our present, and the ever-close-at-hand club of brutality rose and fell on the heads of our people. These images flooded into our home: the vicious fury of bared teeth as mad dogs were set on our people; the pounding, massive pressure of water from hoses flattening and beating our men and women against storefronts or knocking them off their feet; the murdering of four little girls in the bombing of a church, bloodstains saturating their small Sunday gowns. We encountered these images through television and newspapers, but particularly I remember the special dispatches of letters and photographs sent to the home of Jackie Robinson. I was too young to fully understand, but it was clear that my father had celebrated earlier victories, had withstood, and had won respect. And so people came and went, my father came and went on these matters of our race, always matters of our race. My father had played the game of baseball, but baseball seemed of little significance compared to his presence as a man of respect among our people and the problems we were facing.

hese were the years of my childhood, and I had to make my way in these different worlds. I had integrated a school, been called "nigger," and had my few fights, but white people caused me little personal problem. It seemed easy to see that the white children who barked the loudest were the least intelligent of those I schooled with daily. I had seen their homes and parents, and certainly they didn't compare to my own. No, the insults of whites directed at me during my childhood were a passing and minor inconvenience. Much more I was concerned with fishing and reaching the lakes early enough on summer mornings to see the mist floating serenely above the perfectly still water.

During the years of my childhood, my mother took me to see Broadway plays, *The Man of LaMancha* and Sammy Davis, Jr., in *Golden Boy*. Those experiences stand at the base of me like the stones in the foundation of my parents' house. The soundtrack from the play *The Believers*, which I never did see, still haunts my subconscious with the singers' mournful question, "What do we believe in now?"

For me, the answer to that question seemed to exist all around my worlds, and regardless of how long it took to put certain basic understandings in place I was blessed and will be forever thankful for those influences. "We believe in ourselves" was the answer that evolved from my childhood. We believed in our blackness, for although we have always been a people of beauty and substance, the oppression which we persevered against has also forged greatness. My father was struck by more intentionally thrown baseballs than all of his other teammates, and yet he stood and performed and yelled back his challenge to an entire stadium through his taunts to the pitcher while dancing off third base. We are a people who were branded and enslaved for three hundred years, yet we rose to march in the tens of thousands to demand respect in a land of hostility.

I am forty-three years old now in this one world, and although I regret my weaknesses and curse my limited capabilities, I appreciate the lessons my parents and my elders taught me. I have been in the quiet of the forest when the mist is perfect on still water, but until circumstances are set right, what can be will never be. And so we must work, both separately as black people and together as human beings, to effect change.

This book is an effort to remember. I think if we remember and duly respect, we will know both what to believe in and what to do.

David Robinson attended Stanford University, and in 1984 he went to live in Africa. At this writing he and his wife, Ruti, and his children Howard, twins Rachel and Li, and the youngest, Faith, live on their large coffee farm in Imbeya, Tanzania, Africa. His daughters Susan and Ayo attend school in New York and Massachusetts.

SELECTED READING

Allen, Maury. *Jackie Robinson*. New York: Franklin Watts, 1987.

Barber, Red. *1947: When All Hell Broke Loose In Baseball*. New York: DaCapo Press, 1982.

Baseball As We Play It. New York: G.P. Putnam's Sons, 1969.

Cohen, Barbara. *Thank You, Jackie Robinson*. New York: Lothrop, Lee and Shepard, 1974.

Dixon, Phil, and Patrick J. Hannigan. *The Negro Baseball Leagues: A Photographic History*. Mattituck, N.Y.: Amereon House, 1992.

Frommer, Harvey. *Rickey & Robinson*. New York: Macmillan, 1982.

Golenbock, Peter. *Bums: An Oral History of the Brooklyn Dodgers*. New York: G. P. Putnam's Sons, 1994.

_____. *Teammates*. New York: Harcourt Brace Jovanovich, 1990.

Johnson, Spencer. *The Value of Courage*. La Jolla, Cal.: Value Communications, 1977.

Kahn, Roger. *The Boys of Summer*. New York: Harper & Row, 1971 and 1972.

_____. *The Era, 1947–1957: When the Yankees, the Giants and the Dodgers Ruled the World*. New York: Ticknor and Fields, 1993.

Kuhn, Bowie. *Hardball*. New York: Times Books, 1987.

Lord, Bette Bao. *In the Year of the Boar and Jackie Robinson*. New York: Harper & Row, 1984.

Mann, Arthur. *Branch Rickey*. Boston: Houghton Mifflin, 1957.

Mann, Arthur William. *The Jackie Robinson Story*. New York: Grosset and Dunlop, 1956.

Nazel, Joseph G. *Jackie Robinson, First of a Chosen Few*. Los Angeles: Holloway House, 1982.

Olsen, James T. *Jackie Robinson, Pro Ball's First Black Star*. Mankato, Minn.: Creative Education (distr. by Children's Press, Chicago), 1974.

Parrott, Harold. *The Lords of Baseball*. New York: Praeger, 1976.

Riley, James A. *The Biographical Encyclopedia of The Negro Baseball Leagues*. New York: Carroll and Graf, 1994.

Robinson, Jackie. *Baseball Has Done It*. Philadelphia: Lippincott, 1964.

_____. *Breakthrough to the Big League*. New York: Harper & Row, 1965.

_____. *Jackie Robinson's Little League Baseball Book*. Englewood Cliffs, N.J.: Prentice-Hall, 1972.

_____. *I Never Had It Made: An Autobiography*. Hopewell, New Jersey: Ecco Press, repr. 1995.

Roeder, Bill. *Jackie Robinson*. New York: A. S. Barnes & Company, 1950.

Rowan, Carl T., and Jackie Robinson. *Wait Till Next Year*. New York: Random House, 1960.

Scott, Richard. *Jackie Robinson*. Black Americans of Achievement. New York: Chelsea House, 1987.

Shapiro, Milton J. *Jackie Robinson of the Brooklyn Dodgers*. New York: Julian Messner, 1957.

Smith, Wendell, and Jackie Robinson. *Jackie Robinson, My Own Story*. New York: Greenberg, 1948.

Tygiel, Jules. *Baseball's Great Experiment*. New York: Oxford University Press, 1983.

I N D E X

Numbers in *italics* refer to captions and illustrations.

PHOTOGRAPH CREDITS

AP/Wide World Photos: 21 above, 54, 78 below, 85 above right, 91 inset above, 93, 101 above right, 102 above, 104 below left, 106 above, 110–11, 135 center, 137, 147, 149 below, 157 above, 173, 178 below, 179 above, 180 above, 181–82, 206, 215, 218–19; Courtesy Atlantic Records, photo by DAKOTAH: 202; Bagwell Photo: 165; Anthony Calvacca/*New York Post:* 64 below; Camera Associates: 148 below; Campbell & Harper, N.Y., 1947: 65; Chester: 90; Corbis-Bettmann Archive: 39 above right, 58, 64 above, 70, 74 left, 75, 76 above, 79 above, 84–85 center, 92 (Herbie Scharfman), 95, 103 left, 104 below right, 105, 106 below, 107 above, 123 below right, 172, 179 below right, 197 right; Collection Jackie Robinson Foundation: 33, 52, 112, 113, 114 below, 138, 150–51, 168, 210, 226; Courtesy Chock Full O'Nuts: 152, 155 (Wagner International Photos); © Eileen Darby: 99; *Ebony* Magazine-Johnson Publications: 59, 91 inset below, 170, 222 center; *The Evening Bulletin,* Philadelphia: 166; J. R. Eyerman, LIFE Magazine, © Time, Inc.: 61, 98 above right, 114 above left and right, 197 left; Charles Feeney: 47; J. Alan Fisher: 156 below; Monroe S. Frederick II: 186–89, 213 below; Courtesy Grossinger's: 127 above right; Inge Hardison: 134 above; Herbert Hawkins: 79 below, 80 left, 81 right; Courtesy Howard University: 171; Keystone: 89; Layne's Studio: 144–45; Cecil Layne: 179 below left; Nina Leen, LIFE Magazine, © Time, Inc.: 88; *Look* Magazine: 23 below, 131; Courtesy Los Angeles Dodgers: 49, 120, 121 above, 140–41, 212 below, 228; McGonigal: 118; © Chris McNair Studio: 174; Metropolitan News

Service, N.Y.C.: 116–17; Darnell C. Mitchell: 224 inset; Monclova: 185; Allen Morgan: 164, 227; National Baseball Library & Archive, Cooperstown, N.Y.: 23 below, 34, 37, 71–72, 76 below, 96, 121 below, 169 above left; The New York Public Library/Schomburg Center for Research in Black Culture: 225 below; "The News": 98 below; *The New York Eve News:* 108 below; © *Newsday,* photo Ken Spencer: jacket

flap; NYT Pictures: 104 above; *Our World:* 44 above; Powell's Camera Artist: 198 below; Collection Meyer H. Robinson: 78 above; Rachel Robinson: 2, 15–16, 19, 20, 21 below left, 21 right, 22, 25 left, 26, 28, 29 above, 29 center, 29 below, 30, 39 left, 39 below right, 41 (Photo by Joseph), 42 above (Photo by Joseph), 42 below (Photo by Joseph), 43 (Photo by Joseph), 44 below (Photo by Joseph), 45 (Photo by Joseph), 51,

53, 56, 60, 62–63, 68, 74 right, 86, 87 left, 92 above, 92 center, 92 below right, 98 above left, 100, 101 left, 101 below right, 114 below, 124–27 (Photos: Grossinger's), 126, 128, 129–30, 132, 134 below right, 135 below left, 135 below right, 138–39, 149 above, 150, 157 below, 159, 163, 176, 177 below, 184, 185 inset (Photo: Rachel Robinson), 193, 196, 199 above right, 199 below, 204, 205, 209, 211, 212 above, 222 above, 225 above, 233, 234 (Photo: Irwin Simon), 240 (Photo: Rachel Robinson); Reni Photos: 162; Courtesy Rockefeller Papers: 178 above left; Ted Russell, LIFE Magazine, © Time, Inc.: 183; Jerry Saltsberg & Assoc.: 153; Herb Scharfman: 213 above; Paul Schmierer: 87 above right, 112–13; *Sepia* Magazine: 214; © Peter Simon: 133, 134 below left, 235, 236; © Moneta Sleet, Jr./Johnson Publications: 221, 222 below left; P. Smith: 195; Dick Stanley: 198 above; Barney Stein: 67, 69 below left, 69 right, 83, 84 above, 84 below left, 97, 103 right, 108 above, 119, 121 center, 123 center, 146, 154; Barney Stein/*New York Post:* 55, 80–81 center; Ray Stevens: 224; Courtesy Bill Talbert: 139; Frank Tanner: 115; UPI/Corbis-Bettmann: 102 below, 103 left, 123 below, 175, 178 above right, 180 below, 199 above left; Courtesy University of California, Los Angeles: 23, 25 right; Wagner International Photos: 156 above; Bob Weyer: 169 above right, 169 below; Bruce Williams: 191.

The author and the publisher would also like to thank Zindmann/Fremont for making copy-photos: 2, 16 below, 19, 43, 49 below, 52, 69, 91, 102 above, 150–51, 176, 177 above, 196 below, 205 below, 210.

Ayo Robinson, one of my nine lovely grandchildren, quietly celebrating life in the sea breezes of the Indian Ocean.